Oregon's Outback
AN AUTO TOUR GUIDE TO SOUTHEAST OREGON

Donna Lynn Ikenberry

Oregon's Outback

AN AUTO TOUR GUIDE TO SOUTHEAST OREGON

Donna Lynn Ikenberry

Photographs by Donna Lynn Ikenberry

Frank Amato PORTLAND

Dedication

For the late Oral Bullard, a man
who loved God, nature, and life itself.

When I die, I seek no eulogy,
no praise:
No monument to raise its lofty head
in some forgotten town.
I only ask that Spring shall come again
and laughter will be there to greet
each flaming dawn,
That joy and hope and love
will reign
supreme,
When I am gone.

Oral Bullard

Written by Oral Bullard in 1944 when he
thought he was going off to battle. Peace
was declared, however, and Oral never went
to battle. Oral continued to love the spring.

All inquiries should be addressed to:
Frank Amato Publications, Inc.
P.O. Box 82112, Portland, Oregon 97282
Cover Photo: Donna Lynn Ikenberry
All photos by the author.
Book and Cover Design: Kathy Johnson
Printed in Canada

1 3 5 7 9 10 8 6 4 2
ISBN: 1-57188-043-7

Table of Contents

Introduction

When the late Oral Bullard first approached me about writing *Oregon's Outback*, I was thrilled beyond words for I had heard so much about the region. Oral had visited the area many times before and felt a particular fascination with this, the southeast corner of the Beaver State. He loved its beauty, its vastness, its wildlife. He loved the solitude. And it's because of his special love for the region, because of his great kindness toward me and others, because of his love for nature and all its goodness, that I've dedicated this book to him.

I first visited southeast Oregon because of Oral and his contagious love for the place. After talking to him, I had to see what all the commotion was about. What was so spectacular? Why the deep, deep interest?

My first trip to the region answered those questions, and left me hungry to learn more. I could see what Oral found so special. I could understand a person falling in love with the place. It was then that I realized a person hasn't really seen Oregon until they've traveled to the southeast corner.

As a full-time writer and photographer, I'm often asked where I hang out during my travels. And I'm usually pressed into claiming a favorite state. Of course, I speak of Oregon quite often. But when I mention the lovely state, I've noticed that most folks call up images of lush forests and tall, thick trees. Of course, many think of rain and lots of it. The majority of people are surprised when I tell them Oregon is more than just rain, trees, and lots of greenery. The southeast corner is comprised of bone-dry alkali flats, miles upon miles of sagebrush, isolated pockets of aspens and cottonwoods, shallow lakes, glacier-carved gorges, and intense mountains. It's a place where hardy ranchers make use of vast valleys, scraping out a living the best they can. Those with gold on their minds have done the same, working for pennies, toiling and risking their lives in search of the big strike that would leave them set for life.

A variety of animals make this region their home, too. Bighorn sheep, mule deer, mountain lion, and other wildlife inhabit its rugged mountains, vast plains, and the pancake-flat desert. Bald eagles ply azure skies, and trumpeter swans arch their necks gracefully in local lakes, singing a beautiful tune. Rattlesnakes slither and coil, horned lizards burrow into the sand, spiny armor discouraging hungry predators. And if that isn't enough, pronghorn still play, stretching out across sagebrush plains.

Peter Skene Ogden was the first white man to explore the animal-endowed region. Although he happened upon the area in 1825-1826 while leading a fur brigade for the Hudson Bay Company, he found little to brag of in the region and hardly recommended that anyone try and settle the land. Later, during the Idaho gold rush, prospectors came in search of gold, telling tales of fertile ranch and agriculture land. Soon, a number of pioneer ranchers were making a beeline to millions of acres of open bunchgrass plains, homesteading the land and struggling to make ends meet. And while many would-be homesteaders tried to

Road leading to Succor Creek (south of turnoff to Leslie Gulch) on BLM Byway.

scrape out a living and failed, others struggled and survived with several ranches being owned and operated by the same family for many generations. For instance, both the Whitehorse Ranch and the Alvord Ranch began operations in the late 1800s and still operate today.

Before the white man arrived, Native Americans made the region their home. While the nomadic tribes searched for food and shelter, traveling throughout the area, they carved drawings on rocks—petroglyphs—and left behind a series of messages we have yet to comprehend. Before the coming of white settlers, the Northern Paiute Indians led a simple life, eating almost anything that was edible such as roots, berries, seeds, lizards, snakes, insects, marmots, and birds and their eggs. Surprisingly enough, it's also believed they hunted bison.

Most of southeast Oregon rests in the Great Basin, an expansive high desert region particularly noted for its internal drainage system. Here, rain falls, but never reaches the sea. Instead, it either soaks into the ground, or drains into closed valleys where lakes and ponds are formed. Covering about 190,000 square miles, the Great Basin is bordered by the Columbia Plateau on the north, the Mojave Desert on the south, the Wasatch Mountains on the east, and the Sierra Nevada Range on the west.

Rugged mountain blocks—most of which run in a north-south direction—and spacious, intervening valleys, are typical of this region. Formed when massive blocks of the Earth's crust was uplifted, then dropped and tilted, an old survey report likens the mountain ranges to a group of caterpillars, all crawling irregularly northward. Most of the ranges are 60 to 120 miles long and three to 15 miles wide; the valleys are usually somewhat wider than the mountain ranges paralleling them.

Southeast Oregon, as referred to in this guide, includes those areas east of U.S. 395 and south of U.S. 20. It's an area about 160 miles wide and 125 miles long, and includes most of Malheur and Harney Counties, and a small portion of Lake County. (Harney, Lake and Malheur are Oregon's three largest counties covering 28,450 square miles.) This guide also includes a small section of northwest Nevada as State Highway 140 dips down into the state between Adel, Oregon, and Denio, Nevada, passing through the northern section of the Sheldon National Wildlife Refuge before travelers arch back up into Oregon.

Although the main highways are paved for the most part, prepare to negotiate dirt or gravel roads throughout most of the region. Although passenger cars will have no problem on most of the roads mentioned here, those with both a high clearance vehicle and four-wheel drive will find even more opportunities to explore this unique country.

Tourist accommodations are few and far between in this region, although the most populated towns (which I have mentioned) offer all facilities. I've also alluded to the tiny towns offering motels, cafes, groceries, and gas. Campgrounds are listed as well. Camping is available at several Bureau of Land Management (BLM) facilities. For a small fee you'll find picnic tables, grills, water, outhouses, and on occasion, firewood. Primitive camping is the best option if you want to explore fully, as there are countless spots for setting up a camp, with easy access to the area you're most interested in visiting. Private campgrounds with full hookups for recreational vehicles (RVs) are also available in some areas.

When traveling any backroads area, there are certain items you should always carry. In addition to all the usual things like a spare tire, extra automotive belts, oil, et cetera, be sure to carry plenty of water, a first aid kit, extra food, and warm clothing.

This guide is designed with automobile travel in mind, although many of the routes may interest self-contained mountain bikers as well. One mountain biker I spoke with drove down from Washington State, his mountain bike in tow. After dropping his bike off at Fields (a small town at the base of the Pueblo Mountains), he drove to a trailhead. From there, he hiked 20-some odd miles of the Desert Trail. A couple of days later he ended up back at Fields where he promptly mounted his bike and rode

Abert Lake and Abert Rim as seen from U.S. Highway 395.

**Lichen-covered rocks and Warner Peak from jeep trail
south of Hot Springs Camp in the Hart Mountain Antelope Refuge.**

back to the trailhead to pick up his van. His enthusiasm was contagious as he told me his story.

Skinny-tire enthusiasts may want to consider riding some of the paved roads. An avid skinny-tire bicyclist myself, I've dreamed of bicycling some of the paved roads. Unfortunately, I've just never had the time.

Outdoor activities abound in southeast Oregon. Besides biking, favorite things-to-do include rockhounding, photography, wildlife watching, wildflower observation, wind sailing, hang gliding, camping, bathing in a hot springs, hunting, and fishing. Day hiking and backpacking are popular as well. During the winter, snowshoeing, snowmobiling, and cross-country skiing are favored.

Although a hiker's paradise, most of the hiking available in this area is sans maintained trails. But that's half the fun of it. What better way to see the area than to grab a topographic map and compass, pick a point of interest, and take off, making your own trail or perhaps following a game trail to the place of your choosing.

During a recent trip, a friend and experienced cross-country hiker showed me some backcountry areas I never knew existed. While I'd seen much of the region in the past from roads and short, easy-to-follow trails, he guided me into canyons and gorges alive with fall colors. We hiked up glacier-carved gorges enveloped with rimrock, rocky cliffs speckled with various shades of red, orange, and yellow lichen. We stood in awe as our presence frightened two enormous mule deer bucks from a nearly-dry creek bed. And we grabbed for our cameras as a small group of bighorn sheep scrambled up a rocky mountainside led by three big rams.

After several days of cross-country hiking, I've decided it's one of the best ways to see this vast country. I'm also positive it would take nearly a lifetime to do so.

The spaciousness of southeast Oregon is something that cannot be explained. It has to be experienced. For example, Jim Weston, an 87-year-old miner who lives about two dozen miles north of Fields, drives 120 miles one-way to Burns for groceries. When he needs to go to the eye doctor, he takes off to the west and drives 250 miles to Bend. Many of us get our mail delivered directly to our homes. Not Jim. His mailbox is nearly two miles away and delivery is three times a week instead of the usual six.

But Jim Weston is a sturdy man. Although small in stature, Jim is tougher than most. For years, Jim and his younger brother, the late Mike Weston, mined cinnabar using machinery they'd designed and made themselves. Though they never made it big, it's obvious they must have enjoyed trying. The pair built a home into the lower eastern slope of Steens Mountain, nearly burying a quonset hut which offers all the modern conveniences of any home. Jim nukes (microwaves) his food, writes his memoirs on a PC (personal computer), and watches the nightly news on television.

With towns so distant, some of you may be wondering about getting a bath during your visit. No need to worry, as nature has provided an array of refreshing hot springs. There are improved hot springs at Hart Mountain National Antelope Refuge, Sheldon National Wildlife Refuge, and the Alvord Desert, to name a few.

Several more tips for a safe trip include treating all water, unless it's obtained from a reliable source such as a campground or town where the water is potable. If restroom facilities aren't available, make sure you bury (6 to 8 inches deep) all human waste, and pack out or burn (use care when burning) all toilet paper. Of course, you'll want to pack out all trash, including any you might find from a previous visitor. If using the hot springs, do not use soap or shampoo. If you need a shampoo, wash your hair away from the hot springs or any other water source.

Now that all of that's taken care of, all you need to do is pack your things, hop in the car, and take off. It's a place too big to visit in one trip, however, so I'm sure you'll want to go back again. Don't worry, though. It's what all of us southeast Oregon lovers do. We go back again and again and again...

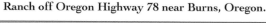

Ranch off Oregon Highway 78 near Burns, Oregon.

Big Indian Gorge
at Steens
Mountain.

Oregon's Outback

Wagontire

Lakeview

Fields

Vale

Plush

BURNS

ROME

Adel

Denio

Lawen

Hines

Fish Lake

Frenchglen

Exploring the Region

Hart Mountain
National Antelope Refuge

Depending on the season, you may enter Hart Mountain National Antelope Refuge and never see a thing. But then again, you may enter the preserve and be treated to one of the greatest wildlife spectacles on earth.

Such was the case recently when I visited the refuge in mid-October. I had been there on previous occasions, sometimes eyeing a pronghorn or two; seeing a small herd of the speedy mammals at other times. However, there were times when I'd see nothing but wide open spaces.

This particular visit made up for all the "slow" days.

Upon entering the Hot Springs Campground, a porcupine waddled by, urging me to snap its portrait. Intent on making some images, I glanced up to see a pair of coyotes ambling along. To my surprise, the porcupine and coyotes continued to greet me as my visit lengthened in the following days.

Off on a day hike one nippy day, two huge, multi-antlered mule deer bucks bid me hello, and then a hasty goodbye as they scampered away. I didn't know it then, but the wildlife extravaganza was just beginning.

An animal-filled week whizzed by. On my last day at the refuge, while visiting Petroglyph Lake, I sat entranced as pronghorn, one spirited herd after another, scurried down to the water for a drink then dashed back up to the rim. Some of the pronghorn stood and watched me, enormous brown eyes twinkling in the sunlight.

Their curiosity was both comical and delightful.

I lingered on the rimrock bordering the west end of the lake, scanning the western horizon with my compact binoculars until darkness was about to engulf me. A herd of about 30 bighorn sheep filled the scene before me, their powerful bodies silhouetted in the setting sun. And then I heard it, the awesome, eerie sound of bighorn rams butting heads. Although it was but a single sound, a headache-inducing smack, I knew it to be but a prelude to the head-butting show that would soon be in full swing. As I walked away from the lake that evening, I reflected on my past days at Hart Mountain National Antelope Refuge. It had been a memorable experience, one I would never forget.

You can make memories of your own upon visiting the preserve which is located 65 miles northeast of Lakeview. With about 275,000 acres to call its own, the refuge was originally set aside in 1936 for the purpose of harboring remnant herds of pronghorn (the sage grouse population was also a concern) which usually ascend upon the area in spring, summer, and fall. Host to some 2,000 pronghorn, the graceful creatures usually retreat in the winter, heading east to Catlow Valley, and 35 miles southeast to Nevada's Sheldon National Wildlife Refuge.

Since its designation, the refuge has expanded to include management of all high-desert wildlife species with bighorn sheep, mule deer, mountain lion, bobcat, coyote, beaver, and badger, sharing space with a variety of smaller mammals such as raccoon, porcupine, skunks, weasels, rabbits, squirrels, and shrews.

Although California bighorn sheep are native to the area, at one time they ceased to be when the last bighorn sheep was shot by hunters early in the 20th century. Of vital importance to early Americans, Indian writings—pictographs and petroglyphs—tell stories of wild sheep hunts. Unfortunately, when the first settlers arrived on the scene, large herds of domestic livestock in tow, the sheep's demise was but a matter of time. Overhunted, in competition with domestic livestock for forage, prone to introduced diseases, the bighorns all but disappeared by the early 1900s.

In September 1939, the first reintroduction program was installed with 23 Rocky Mountain bighorn sheep (seven males, 13 females, and three lambs) being transplanted from the National Bison Range in Montana. The sheep didn't survive. In November 1954, the Oregon State Game Commission joined forces with the U.S. Fish and Wildlife Service (who administers the refuge), and transplanted 20 California bighorn sheep *(Ovis canadensis californiana)* furnished by British Columbia. The plan was a huge success and by the 1980s, the bighorn sheep, which live in the area all year and number about 450, extended their range.

Look for the sheep along the steep western slopes from a point below Hart Canyon to Poker Jim Ridge, a distance of 15 miles. Stop at any location along the road leading from Plush and you may see sheep traversing the extensive cliffs of the upper slope. The primary nursery is found along these cliffs, providing binocular-clad visitors with the opportunity to observe ewes and lambs. This is particularly true during the spring and summer when ewes and lambs frequent the area.

Hiking is perhaps the best way to see the sheep which live in the area year-round. If a day trip is all you have time for, try Degarmo and Arsenic Canyons. Both areas are used extensively by rams during summer and early fall. If you have time for an overnight trip, try the southern half of Hart Mountain during summer. (Backpackers must obtain a free self-registration permit at Refuge Headquarters or the Lakeview Office.) If visiting the northern half of Hart Mountain, including Poker Jim Ridge, you'll

Campground at Antelope Reservoir, off U.S. 95, west of Jordan Valley.

**Pickup descending road to Plush
en route to Hart Mountain Antelope Refuge.**

have the best luck if you hike to the top of the ridge and use a scope or binoculars to locate the sheep along the cliff areas. If hiking the area in May and early June, please refrain from entering the cliff areas so as not to disturb tiny lambs.

Look for mule deer anytime of the year (please note, deer will migrate out of the area during severe winters) at the refuge, although spring and summer are best for viewing. From 800 to 1,000 mule deer live on Hart Mountain and the Intermediate Hills. As with most mammals, early morning and late afternoon are the best times to view the animals as they are moving about feeding. Look for deer in or near aspen and junipers; does stick around riparian areas during summer.

Bird populations are impressive as well with over 264 species recorded on Hart Mountain and in the adjacent Warner Valley, part of which is located in the refuge itself. Much of the heavy waterfowl and waterbird migrations occur in Warner Valley with the greatest concentrations visible in spring and fall. During the spring, summer, and fall, watch for sage grouse, a variety of

smaller birds, and various species of birds of prey (including golden eagles and prairie falcons) which flock to the rugged cliffs and spring-fed riparian areas. Others find refuge on the vast sagebrush and grassland plains.

Several amphibians also make the refuge their home. These include the Pacific tree frog and the western toad. Reptiles consist of a variety of lizards and several types of snakes including the western rattlesnake.

Hart Mountain National Antelope Refuge is more than animal life, however. It's the chance to explore off trail, it's solitude, it's lounging the day away in a hot springs, or photographing a variety of old cabins. It's imagining life at the old Shirk Ranch. It's the opportunity for fishing one of two quiet streams, and the chance to just sit back and enjoy the scenery.

Hart Mountain is easy to look at. A massive fault block ridge for which the refuge was named, Hart Mountain is the highest mountain on the eastern edge of Warner Valley, rising 8,065 feet into the heavens at a point atop Warner Peak. To the north, the extremely steep scarp known as Poker Jim Ridge is lower in height, but no less dramatic. The result of what geologists call block faulting, this mountain, as well as others like it, formed from a mass of rock that was uplifted and then tilted. Like much of the Great Basin landscape, the mountain is composed of lava.

Approach the mountain from the east and you'll hardly notice the climb as gentle rolling hills and low ridges slope upward from Catlow Valley, slowly rising to a wide sagebrush-covered plateau where you'll find several lakes, Refuge Headquarters and a road leading to the Hot Springs Campground. Enter from the west, the most dramatic approach, and you'll climb some 3,600 feet from the floor of the lake-blessed Warner Valley, passing several, rugged, steep-sided canyons—Hart, Potter, and DeGarmo—en route.

Although the lake-blessed Warner Valley doesn't always appear so endowed (it may be dry and barren at times, particularly during drought years), Hart Mountain has been referred to as "an oasis in the desert" and with good reason. Many fine springs enrich the area. Rock Creek and Guano Creek provide more than liquid refreshment for thirsty wildlife. They are open for public fishing as well, with introduced Lahontan cutthroat trout plying the waters of Guano Creek: Native redband trout live in Rock Creek.

Habitat types are as diverse as the land itself, varying from big and low sagebrush which blankets much of the area, to mountain mahogany and bitterbrush, found primarily in the regions above 6,000 feet. Secluded canyons provide safe harbor for aspen, as well as, snowbrush, wild gooseberry, and chokecherry. A select group of pines take refuge in one section of the preserve. Grassy spring-fed meadows, juniper-covered uplands, marshes and alkaline lakes also exist.

If you're interested in plants and learning more about them, be sure to walk around the native plant display near Refuge Headquarters. You'll see species such as basin wild-rye, the most predominant bunch grass on the refuge, and low sagebrush. Rarely reaching heights of more than two feet, low sagebrush is an important yearly browse and protein source for both pronghorn and sage grouse. Think of southeast Oregon and you'll most certainly think of big sagebrush which is also represented

Bighorn sheep at Leslie Gulch.

Aspens in the fall at Hot Springs Campground, Hart Mountain National Antelope Refuge.

here. Other plant species in the display include tapertip hawksbeard, rough fescue, Idaho fescue, Indian ricegrass, bitterbrush, bluebunch wheatgrass, and arrowleaf balsamroot.

Wildflowers can be abundant in spring, especially if generous rains have graced the region. With the proper condi-

tions, Hart Mountain is a potpourri of scented delights as monkey flowers, phlox, starflowers, paintbrush, and multi-colored violets add to the lush scene. The season usually extends from February when the first buttercups brighten lower elevations, to September when the last of the golden-rods and gentians grace the meadows along the mountain top. Look for a variety of other species in the months and elevations in between.

Facilities are limited at Refuge Headquarters which is comprised of a series of stone buildings built by Civilian Conservation Corp (CCC) workers in the 1930s. There's a restroom adjacent to the visitor room; water is also available. Open 24 hours a day, the visitor room is not handicapped accessible, nor are any of the other restroom facilities at the preserve. The small town of Plush, located approximately 25 miles west, offers the nearest amenities—gas, a phone, water, and groceries. Adel, located about 45 miles south of Hart Mountain offers the same in addition to an RV park and a post office.

Camping is by far the best way to stay and explore the refuge as facilities such as hotels, restaurants, and markets are nonexistent in the refuge itself. Those who crave more luxurious sleeping arrangements may want to check out the Frenchglen Hotel in downtown Frenchglen, a tiny hamlet about 49 miles to the northeast. Reservations are recommended.

Camping facilities are primitive at the refuge—there are pit toilets and a few picnic tables. Suitable for tents and campers, the sites aren't designed for long recreational vehicles (RVs). RVs of limited length may find room to park at the Hot Springs Campground, but sites at the Guano Creek Campground are not appropriate. Those in need of ample space or hookups should park their rigs at the Steens Mountain Resort, a private campground with full hookups, or the Page Springs Campground, a BLM campground sans hookups, near Frenchglen.

The Hot Springs Campground is open year-round. Located four miles south of Refuge Headquarters, sites are located in a depression of sorts with Rock Creek meandering through, providing nourishment for an array of willows and shrubs. Aspens also grace the area, their leaves rattling a golden goodbye come fall. Named for the hot springs bathhouse which has seen the sweat and grime of more than one grateful body,

the springs are enclosed in a cement building for privacy.

Guano Creek Campground is located to the south, although it is only open during hunting season. Whereas I think the practice of keeping the campground closed except for hunting season is unfortunate, I'd recommend a visit. Check with Refuge Headquarters for opening and closing dates.

En route to the Guano Creek Campground you'll pass what is known as "Blue Sky," a stately forest of ponderosa pines. Surrounded by high desert, the lush green haven was the scene of the week-long annual meeting of The Order of the Antelope, a group formed by local businessmen responsible for lobbying Congress to establish the refuge. Although they continue to lobby for funding, the controversial meetings are no longer allowed on refuge land. However, refuge manager Barry Reiswig reports the group "has purchased a private inholding on the refuge and intend to hold their blowout there." Reiswig states that such action must first be approved by LCDC and meet provisions of the Oregon Land Use Law.

These pines were also the site of Camp Warner, a U.S. Army military post, established in 1866 under the leadership of General Crook. Although the first white men had set foot in the region prior to that (in 1843 members of the Fremont Expedition explored the area), by the 1860s settlers ventured forth to graze their livestock on fertile grasslands. Their homeland threatened, the Indians naturally rebelled, murdering families, burning homes, and scattering livestock. Under the leadership of General Crook, Camp Warner was established.

Unfortunately, Camp Warner was a frigid hell for the men who served here during the winter of 1866-67. Historical documents describe a cruel, severe winter for those staying at the camp located at the 6,500-foot level. Suffering due to deep snows and frigid temperatures, General Crook ordered his soldiers to relocate the camp, and on July 29, 1867, the company

Shirk Ranch in the Hart Mountain National Antelope Refuge.

moved to a site at a lower elevation to the west of the Warner Valley. Several years later, General Crook accomplished the task of suppressing the Indians, and area ranchers settled the region.

The area hardly seems settled, however. When visiting the refuge, allow extra traveling time as paved roads are nonexistent. Graded roads lead into the refuge from the east and west, as well as, the Hot Springs Campground. Blue Sky Road (closed in the winter and spring to reduce disturbance to wildlife and because of hazardous road conditions) is also graded and leads to the Blue Sky area and Guano Creek Campground. Jeep trails dissect much of the refuge, piloting one to specific points such as Petroglyph Lake. Four wheel drive and high clearance vehicles are often nec-

essary as the jeep trails can be very rough. Watch for jeep trail closures. Many of the trails are permanently closed: Some close seasonally to reduce wildlife disturbance and road damage.

Favored refuge activities include searching for petroglyphs, or Indian rock carvings. Interested? You'll find plenty of petroglyphs located on shallow rimrocks throughout the plateau and lakebed region. Look for the carvings on the large boulders along Campbell and Hart Lakes located at the base of Hart Mountain, and along the rimrock at Petroglyph Lake. Please remember, though, that no archeological artifacts (this includes arrowheads) may be disturbed or collected. Artifacts found on Federal lands are protected by the Archeological Resource Protection Act.

Rockhounding is also a popular activity. Please note, there's a limit of seven pounds of rock specimens per person. Of course, blasting and digging are prohibited.

Hunting is also an annual highlight for many folks. Special hunting seasons are provided with "emphasis placed on quality hunting experiences" according to refuge literature. As mentioned previously, fishing is available in Rock and Guano Creeks, as well as Warner Pond. An Oregon license is required. Check with Refuge Headquarters for more information regarding both activities.

Hiking is perhaps the best way to explore this unique area. While maintained trails are nonexistent, there are plenty of old roads to follow, and game trails often provide entry into the unknown. Armed with all the necessities for either a day hike or an extended backpack trip, a topographic map close at hand, you can hike to the top of Warner Peak for a sweeping view of your surroundings, explore one or more of the canyons gracing the area, or spend time examining one of several old cabins. Highly intriguing, deeply mystifying, a photographer could spend days making pictures of these old cabins, visiting each spot in a different season, capturing the essence of a time that was.

If buildings are your thing, if imagining the past—the gunfights, the wildly-unconstrained men that made up this land—are your thing, then you'll want to make one last stop before exiting the refuge for points beyond. Because for you, the Shirk Ranch is a must-see.

Located in an isolated pocket to the south of the bulk of the Hart Mountain National Antelope Refuge, about 12 miles north of State Highway 140, the historic Shirk Ranch is a mishmash of delightful old buildings.

Homesteaded by R.A. Turner in the early 1880s, the Guano Valley land was later deeded to William Herron. In 1887, David Shirk bought 850 acres of the ranch, managing its operations and development until 1914 when the ranch was purchased by Lake County Land and Livestock Company.

Shirk was a horse and cattle man, and also the author of *The Cattle Drives of David Shirk,* an autobiography about life in southeastern Oregon, and cattle drives which spanned from Texas to Oregon. In 1888, Shirk killed a "land grabber" by the name of James Issacs. Acting in self-defense, Shirk was acquitted and eventually left Oregon in the early 1900s, but he couldn't stay away. Up until 1914, when the ranch was sold out, Shirk spent his summers at the ranch.

Although there were some ownership changes in the ensuing years, the ranch was purchased for the last time in 1942 for inclusion as part of the Hart Mountain National Antelope Refuge.

While some of the buildings, including the original ranch house, were nailed together sometime between about 1870 and 1890, the unique ranch house seen today and some of the other buildings were built about 1910. Several other outbuildings were added shortly thereafter. According to a U.S. Fish and Wildlife Service report, the buildings that still exist represent "an excellent example of late 19th-and turn-of-the-century rural building types."

Unfortunately, the buildings are deteriorating, furniture is missing, and a long barn has been destroyed. The scene is heartbreaking for area historians. And while refuge authorities agree there is a problem, a lack of funds prohibits doing much to change the situation as there is neither money for preservation or restoration. Still, the buildings are worth a look.

Each year some 17,000 visitors come to explore the Hart Mountain National Antelope Refuge. Whereas the refuge is open year-round, most folks visit between Memorial Day and Labor Day. Mid-May through October is the best season to visit the refuge, although you should be prepared for chilly, if not downright cold temperatures. Winters can be frigid and roads may be temporarily closed due to rain and snow.

For further information contact the Hart Mountain National Antelope Refuge. (See page 86 for address.)

Jordan Valley Area

As a full-time traveler and self-proclaimed "desert rat", I must admit to exploring many remarkable places, some of which I long to visit time and time again. Leslie Gulch, Succor Creek, the Owyhee River, and Lake Owyhee are at the top of my "places-to-go-again" list for this fall. Like a bowl of frozen yogurt, this area is so tasty, so sinfully delicious, it's almost too good to be true.

Located near the Idaho border, south of the Vale/Ontario (Oregon) area and west of the Nampa/Caldwell (Idaho) area, the Leslie Gulch, Succor Creek, and Owyhee regions are sometimes referred to as "ION Country," named quite frankly because Idaho, Oregon and Nevada convene there, meeting in the immense wonders of this wildly open region.

Whatever you choose to call it, there's no doubt that it's a land rich in contrast. There are unique geologic formations—deep, narrow gorges, some with 1,000-foot sheer-rock walls, arches, balanced rocks, multicolored spires, towering cliffs, and rolling uplands. Wide, sweeping views of Three Fingers Rock, Lake Owyhee (Oregon's longest lake at 53 miles), Mahogany Mountain, and Owyhee Ridge, add to the scene.

Much of the region is accessible via the 52-mile Leslie Gulch-Succor Creek National Back Country Byway, one of many designated Bureau of Land Management (BLM) byways. Folks at BLM insist that these areas "provide access to a diversity of landscapes and attractions just waiting to be rediscovered."

You'll travel throughout the area via county and BLM graded dirt and graveled roads. Please note, the roads are not maintained during the winter months and should not be traveled when wet or snowy. Mid-April through October is typically the best time for travel, although roads may be temporarily impassable due to flash floods, et cetera. Whereas the roads are usually accessible for those with a typical family vehicle, a high clearance two-wheel drive vehicle is recommended. Large recreational vehicles are strongly discouraged due to steep and narrow terrain. The upper part of Leslie Gulch Canyon, for example, sports an 11 percent grade.

Allow plenty of time for a safe, unhurried journey. Visit in May and early June and you'll no doubt be witness to a profusion of colorful wildflowers. If you're into rare plants, there are two endemic species to look for—Packard's blazing star and Etter's grounsel. Days are usually comfortable with lots of sunshine. Be prepared, however, for all types of weather when traveling in this part of the country.

The Byway passes through the Leslie Gulch Area of Critical Environmental Concern (ACEC), selected for its engaging wildlife, exceptional vegetation, and striking scenery. Three wilderness study areas border the Byway—Honeycombs, Slocum Creek, and Upper Leslie Gulch. Also, the Byway passes through Succor Creek State Recreation Area, an area that boasts of petrified wood and Oregon's state rock, the agate-filled thunderegg.

Dedicated wildlife watchers may spot bobcat, badger, otter, marmot, porcupine, rabbit, coyote, mule deer, pronghorn, mountain lion, and California bighorn sheep. Bighorn sheep were reintroduced into the Leslie Gulch area in 1965. Since then, a herd of 17 sheep has increased to well over 200 individuals. Other wildlife includes a variety of reptiles (some think of them as creepy crawlers) such as collared, leopard, and desert horned lizards, hairy scorpions, and western rattlesnakes which are fairly common throughout the area. Rattlesnakes are also the only poisonous creatures you'll have to watch out for.

Pony Express Station at Arock.

Respect them, give them a wide berth, and you shouldn't have any problems.

Bird life is abundant as well. Upland game birds include chukar and California quail which haunt the canyonlands, while a number of raptors ply the deep, blue skies. The Owyhee River Canyon is a favored nesting site for many raptors. Common species include Swainson's, ferruginous, red-tailed, and northern harrier hawks. Also, there are American kestrels, prairie falcons, and sharp-shinned hawks which frequent the area. North America's largest birds of prey also inhabit the region. Golden eagles live here year-round and bald eagles stay the winter.

Wintering waterfowl often swim around in the unfrozen pools found between rapids. More than 3,000 geese have been tallied, with nearly as many mallard, redhead, scaup, merganser, teal, and grebe visible.

The natural history of the region is perhaps as, if not more, exciting than the wildlife itself. Unlike most of the areas covered in this guide, this region is usually not considered a true part of the Great Basin, although many plants and animals are typical of the Great Basin Desert. While the Great Basin consists of land-locked High Desert, a place where its waters never reach the sea, the Owyhee River does flow outward to the ocean via the Snake and Columbia River drainages.

On its way to the sea, the Owyhee River has cut a path 500 to 1,100 feet deep into the high plateau of the Owyhee Uplands, carving a series of sauntering, U-shaped canyons, vertical walls, and precipitous talus slopes en route. Of volcanic origin, the plateau averages 5,000 feet in elevation and is flat to gently rolling.

Millions of years ago this region was of a cooler, wetter clime, with a relic stand of ponderosa pine at Leslie Gulch testimony to that time. Don't expect to visit the unique stand, however. Rich Conrad, BLM Vale District, claims visitors cannot explore this small stand of about 30 small trees because there's a section of private land which is off

Dirt road leading through Leslie Gulch.

limits to those venturing into the side canyon where the trees are located.

However, you can see extensive lava beds and a number of warm springs which grace the area, evidence of a time when things heated up significantly. Of volcanic origin, you'll find the oldest exposed rocks in the Succor Creek Formation, formed about 15 million years ago. The Leslie Gulch Tuff is a member of this formation and unique within the Owyhee region. According to geologists, "As a rhyolite ash-flow tuff up to 1,000 feet thick, it erupted from a volcanic vent, Mahogany Mountain, as a very mobile molten froth filled with hot volcanic gases. This tuff is best displayed in Leslie Gulch as steep slopes and vertical pitted towers and pinnacles resulting from differential erosion."

Explore the talus slopes of the Leslie Gulch ash-flow tuff and you may find several rare plant species. Grimy ivesia, an extremely rare perennial (in Oregon), inhabits only three sites in the canyon. Two species—Packard's blazing star and Etter's grounsel—are found only in the Leslie Gulch drainage.

Hike some of the side canyons, and you'll most likely find evidence of Native Americans, the first humans not only to discover, but to inhabit the region. Modern-day hikers often "discover" smoke-blackened ceilings under rock overhangs and inside caves, evidence of fires built by what was primarily the Paiute bands of long ago. Numerous petroglyphs and pictographs yield evidence to these first inhabitants.

While some believe Native Americans may have inhabited the Owyhee Uplands as early as 12,000 years ago, recorded history of this region by the white man began in 1812. The name Owyhee, however, developed a few years later when an 1818 Northwest Fur Company scouting expedition entered the area under the direction of Donald McKenzie. From the headwaters of the Owyhee River (which lies in what is now southwestern Idaho), McKenzie sent two (some reports state three) Hawaiian crew members down the river into present-day Oregon. They never returned. The untamed canyon was named in their honor, using the South Sea pronunciation for their home islands, "Owyhee."

As was typical throughout the American West, conflicts arose as the white man came in search of gold. Later, cattle and sheep ranches were established and Native Americans were cast aside. Understandably, the Paiutes rebelled and U.S. Army troops established several military camps in the region to crush hostilities.

Today's visitors enjoy some of the same opportunities as those who both visited and settled the land a long time ago. Activities include hiking, swimming, fishing, hunting, camping, and rockhounding. Photography is also popular, as is kayaking, rafting, and drift boating.

Corrals at Three Forks.

A float-trip down the river (portions of which are included in the National Wild and Scenic Rivers System) is "the best and sometimes the only way to see it," according to Rich Conrad, as road-access is minimal.

This is especially true if you're anxious to explore the cramped, steep-walled gorges of this river which is recognized as a prime early-season white water river.

Only experienced river-runners should consider floating the river. From Three Forks to Rome, the river is very challenging with two to four days required to negotiate this tough 39-mile section of river. Referred to as a "drop and pool" river, there are long sections of flat water interrupted by difficult Class III, IV and V+ rapids.

From Rome to Owyhee Reservoir, boaters float 67 miles, and do so in four to six days. This is the most popular section of the river, also known as a "drop and pool" type, with numerous Class II and III rapids challenging those floating in rafts, drift boats, canoes, and kayaks.

Spring runoff from March through June marks the normal float season. Boaters should be prepared for severe fluctuations in water level and severe weather conditions, including rain, snow, and strong winds. Those parties planning a float trip must register with the Bureau of Land Management prior to the trip. Registration boxes are located at the Rome and Three Forks Launch Sites. For more information regarding campsites, launch sites, shuttles, and river ethics, ask for the "Owyhee National Wild River Boating Guide" available from the BLM, Vale District.

Professional float-trip guides offer complete adventure packages for the inexperienced. For more information contact the Idaho Outfitters Guide Association, P.O. Box 95, Boise, ID 83701; (208) 342-1919 and/or the Oregon Guides and Packers Association, P.O. Box 10841, Eugene, OR 97440; (541) 683-9552.

For more information contact the Bureau of Land Management, Vale District. (See page 86 for address.)

Malheur National Wildlife Refuge

Malheur National Wildlife Refuge has always conjured up images of a vast avian population for me. For years I listened as others spoke of trumpeter swans and immense flocks of ducks and geese. I vowed that one day I would make it over to the refuge to stand in awe of the bird life around me.

I finally visited the refuge a couple of years ago and I was not disappointed. It was everything I had hoped it would be. And more. I saw trumpeter swans bobbing upon refuge waters, their long, elegant necks dipping under the surface to feed, their giant webbed feet kicking at nothing but air. Listening to the gentle murmur of these, the largest swans in North America, I was certain the peaceful sound must be drifting up into the heavens.

Great horned owls were my daily companions as I explored the cottonwood trees lining Benson Pond. I observed several of the sleepy creatures everyday. Sometimes I'd stay until nightfall so I could watch the owls emerge from the safety of their perch and fly out to earn their reputation as "tigers of the night."

With nearly 186,000 acres to call its own, I discovered that Malheur National Wildlife Refuge, one of the largest of more than 475 units within the National Wildlife Refuge System, is definitely a birder's mecca. But it's more than just 300 species of birds, it's 58 species of mammals, too. It's critters like mule deer, porcupine, and many others, including the playful river otter.

Trapped out in the 1930s, otters were reintroduced back into the refuge between 1982 and 1984 when the Oregon Department of Fish and Wildlife released eight river otters. According to Beth Ullenberg, Outdoor Recreation Planner for the refuge, "In the last three years several otters have been sighted on the Refuge. Staff biologists believe there are at least three to four otters and maybe more still residing here."

The refuge was originally designated in 1908 when President Theodore Roosevelt signed legislation into effect establishing the refuge to protect a nesting colony of herons, egrets, cormorants and ibis. Hunted to near extinction in the early part of this century, the plumes of these birds (as well as those of swans and grebes) were used for the millinery trade. Today these birds are protected and the refuge provides a safe refuge for an abundance of animal life including the endangered peregrine falcon.

The Blitzen und Donner National Wild and Scenic River meanders through the heart of the preserve. A German name which translates to thunder and lightning, the river was named by Captain George B. Currey who led his men across the river during a thunderstorm in 1864.

Several tributary creeks join the Blitzen River in its quest for Malheur Lake, the largest freshwater marsh in the western United States. The Blitzen Valley portion of the refuge has been intensively developed with an assortment of man-made canals, dikes, and ponds, generating habitat that is attractive to both wildlife and nature fans.

Great horned owl. Malheur National Wildlife Refuge.

View to the east (Mann Lake in background)
from the East Rim. Steens Mountain.

Extending 35 miles from Page Springs to Malheur Lake, the narrow valley is the most accessible portion of the refuge and covers roughly 66,000 acres. A birding bonanza, it's been said that nearly every species on the refuge can be seen between Refuge Headquarters and Frenchglen. Of course, visitors shouldn't expect to see them all in one day.

The Donner und Blitzen River joins a series of lakes, alkali flats, irrigated meadows, rimrock, and grass and sagebrush-covered hills, in forming a region where the animal life is as diverse as the land itself. The heart of the refuge is made up of a complex of vast lakes called the Malheur-Harney Lakes Basin (also called Oregon Closed Basin). Located at the northern edge of the Great Basin, these lakes (including smaller Mud Lake) do not drain into the sea. Instead, water escapes only by evapotranspiration, a term Webster's describes as the "loss of water from the soil both by evaporation and by transpiration from the plants growing thereon."

Water flows into the nucleus of the region—the three lakes—by an equal number of major water systems. Silvies River is born in the Blue Mountains and drains into the north end of the complex at Malheur Lake; Silver Creek originates in the Blue Mountains as well, emptying into the northwest corner of Harney Lake. Entering the refuge from the south end, the Donner und Blitzen River makes its onstage appearance on the western slopes of Steens Mountain, and also empties into Malheur Lake.

With amounts of precipitation a regular guessing game from one year to the next, the refuge is a land of constant change. And most of this change is either due to too much or too little water. In the early 1930s there was a severe drought and Malheur Lake dried up completely. Cars ambled across the dry lakebed at will, with all river water being diverted for irrigation and none of it emptying into the lake.

In the early 1980s, the opposite occurred when flood waters inundated the area. Nearby mountains felt the weight of three years of heavy snowpack and shrugged the burden off thereby flooding the Malheur-Harney Lakes Basin. Harney, Mud, and Malheur Lakes swelled to an estimated 180,000 acres, joining together like one large inland sea. In fact, this sea was so large that when all three lakes joined together they became Oregon's largest body of inland water.

While the land may change from year to year, the local animal life usually changes with the seasons. Most of the mammals live here year-round; some species of birds live here all year as well.

Located on the Pacific Flyway, one of four major migration routes in North America, the refuge is a birding hotspot come spring and fall. In the spring, look for the waterfowl migration which peaks in late March. Visit during this season and you'll observe large flocks of ducks, geese, tundra swans, and lesser sandhill cranes. (Reported numbers boast of more than 250,000 ducks, 125,000 geese, and nearly 10,000 lesser sandhill cranes.)

Although resident trumpeter swans are seen in limited numbers (about 60 birds frequent the area; 12 to 15 pairs nest regularly), you'll see large quantities of tundra swans in spring and autumn. The nearly identical birds are uncommon in winter, however, as they migrate farther south, and they're rare in summer as they opt to nest in the Far North.

In April, the refuge is inundated with a variety of shorebirds. Songbird numbers peak around the middle of May with the best places to observe the migratory bird population being Page Springs, P Ranch, and Refuge Headquarters. Actually, the songbird hotspot is usually found at the lawn and woodlot at Refuge Headquarters when spring migration is at its peak.

Summer visitors will enjoy the year-round residents, those creatures that nest and raise their young here. These include a variety of ducks, great horned owls, golden eagles, Canada geese, herons, pelicans, ibis, and terns to name a few. If you're into turkey vultures, visit the P Ranch during the summer and you'll see large numbers of these bare-headed birds gathered atop the metal tower. After congregating at the ranch in the afternoon, the birds fly to adjacent cottonwoods to roost.

While spring is definitely the best time to see mega-quantities of birds, fall can also be quite rewarding. In September and October, the fall migration begins with great numbers of ducks, geese, and greater sandhill cranes joining together to feed in the Blitzen Valley grain fields. Actually, greater sandhill cranes are abundant from spring through fall as the pairs, which establish life-long bonds, nest on the refuge.

Winters bring cold temperatures, but it is a good time to look for the birds that have flocked to small pockets of open water. It is also a good time to observe rough-legged hawks, bald eagles, and trumpeter swans.

The Paiute Indians must have seen scenes such as these for this area was a favored wintering spot for the Native

Americans. Both Malheur and Harney Lakes were permanent wintering homes for the Wada Tika, a band of Paiute Indians who roamed throughout central and southern Oregon. A nomadic tribe, the Indians traveled in family units or clans, wandering great distances in search of food and shelter. Forced off their land when the white man moved onto the scene, many of the Wada Tika descendants now live on the Burns Paiute Indian Reservation located north of Burns.

Additional evidence of early Native Americans surfaced after the disastrous floods of the early 1980s. It was during this time that Malheur Lake reached its highest level in over 100 years. When the high waters finally receded, a barren shoreline was exposed to the ravages of mighty winds which blasted away at the soil, uncovering ancient burial sites, as well as, lodges, and roasting and food storage areas. Unfortunately, an influx of "pothunters" (commercial treasure seekers) and diggers flocked to the area destroying some of the sites. Remember, it is against the law to disturb or collect any archeological artifacts (this includes arrowheads). Artifacts found on Federal lands are protected by the Archeological Resource Protection Act.

As mentioned previously, the P Ranch is a good spot for birding. Now part of the refuge, the ranch was once headquarters of the Peter French cattle empire. Working for a wealthy California rancher by the name of Dr. Hugh James Glenn, French emerged

Lawen Market/Post Office, Lawen, Oregon.

Peter French Round Barn east of Malheur National Wildlife Refuge.

onto the local scene in 1872 with a herd of cattle and six Mexican vaqueros. (Nearby Frenchglen was named for both French and Glenn.) He quickly expanded his cattle operation, enlarging his holdings to over 100,000 acres, 30,000 head of cattle, and 3,000 horses and mules within the next 25 years. French ran large herds of half-wild cattle on the open range, combining this Texas tradition with that of the English methods of stock farming. In 1883, French married Glenn's oldest daughter, Ella. Seventeen days later, Glenn was killed. Huram Miller did the dirty deed on February 17, 1883. Fourteen years later, Peter French was also murdered. Ed Oliver, a disgruntled neighbor, killed French on December 26, 1897.

French's clever construction techniques are visible to those who come to explore the P Ranch. Built in the 1880s, a long barn, beef wheel, and several willow and stockade fences are all that remains of the once prosperous ranch. (This is all that remains of the ranch at this particular site. For a unique treat, visit the Peter French Round Barn. For more information see the Burns/Malheur Refuge/Diamond Craters loop tour.)

While birding is definitely the most favored refuge activity, both hunting and fishing are popular activities, as well. Anglers try primarily for rainbow trout and black bass in areas that include Krumbo Reservoir and Krumbo Creek (above the reservoir), Bridge and Mud Creeks, and portions of the Donner und Blitzen River and Canal. Hunters vie for geese, ducks, coots, snipes, pigeons, chukars, Hungarian partridge, pheasants, quail, dove, pronghorn, deer, coyotes, and rabbits. Hunting and fishing are subject to applicable State and Federal laws; contact Refuge Headquarters for more information.

Those with a yearning to learn more about the refuge and the local animal life should contact the Malheur Field Station (MFS), located four miles west of headquarters. A variety of classes, workshops, and events are offered, ranging from the landscapes and biota of Steens Mountain, to outdoor photography, to field ethnobotany,

and much more. The MFS Nature Hostel is open year-round, with dormitories and family housing available for individuals, groups, or conferences of up to 200 participants. Also, there are a limited number of trailer hookups; reservations recommended. In addition to a dining hall, there are cooking facilities, a recreation room and gym, a library, and a laundry room. For more information write or call: Malheur Field Station, HCR 72, Box 260, Princeton, OR 97721; (541) 493-2629.

Frenchglen Hotel. Frenchglen, Oregon.

Pond at Malheur National Wildlife Rufuge.

Although camping is not available on the refuge itself, you'll find two campgrounds located near the southern boundary. These include Page Springs, a BLM campground, and Steens Mountain Resort, a private campground. The nearest motel accommodations are in Frenchglen (reservations recommended) and Burns. Frenchglen is a quaint hamlet about one mile west of the P Ranch, and about 60 miles south of Burns. The tiny town consists of the hotel, a general store/post office, and a school. Burns is a full-facility town (there are campgrounds as well) located about 36 miles north of Refuge Headquarters.

When visiting the area, most of which is located at about 4,100 feet in elevation, expect a climate typical of the Intermountain West. In other words, be prepared for hot summers and cold winters. Precipitation is usually light, about nine inches a year. Summer thunderstorms may produce some hail, with spectacular lightning shows sometimes visible.

While State Highway 205 which leads to the refuge and on to Frenchglen is paved, the last six miles of road to Refuge Headquarters is gravel. Roads throughout the refuge are gravel as well, so be prepared to travel long distances over unpaved roads. In addition to the usual items (a tank full of gas, water, et cetera), I'd suggest bringing insect repellent if visiting during the spring and summer.

You'll find Refuge Headquarters, open weekdays from 8 a.m. to 4:30 p.m., on the south shore of Malheur Lake. The George M. Benson Memorial Museum is also located at headquarters. Nearly 200 mounted bird specimens make bird identification a bit easier to bear for some visitors. The museum is open daily from 6:00 a.m. to 9:00 p.m.

For additional information contact the Malheur National Wildlife Refuge. (See page 86 for address.)

Sheldon National Wildlife Refuge

One fall day I stood among the spacious high desert plains, trying to imagine the land as it was millions of years ago. Instead of dry, it was soggy; instead of what some would call barren, it was lush. Today, the area receives six to 13 inches of precipitation. Then, the climate was milder with an annual rainfall exceeding 50 inches.

If I could travel back to the mid-Miocene time period, about 20 million years ago, I would no doubt stand in awe of the plant and animal life before me. Although it's difficult to picture, I would see a landscape of grasslands and pine forests. And I'd observe ancient antelope, camels, three-toed horses, giant pigs, and saber-toothed cats, roaming the land. If you were there, you'd see the same.

Tough to envision? It is for most people. It was for me. But it's true, and you can explore this land when you visit Nevada's Sheldon National Wildlife Refuge.

Although this guidebook is focused primarily on southeast Oregon, I've included the Sheldon National Wildlife Refuge for several reasons. First of all, when venturing from Adel, Oregon, to Denio, Nevada (Denio is located on the California/Nevada border), I found State Highway 140 to be the quickest and easiest route from one town to the next. Because the highway passes through the northern part of the refuge, I decided to include it. Second, many of the pronghorn that winter in this area also live in Oregon, migrating south from points in Oregon (see the chapter on Hart Mountain National Antelope Refuge for more information). As a result, I thought it only fitting to include this refuge in *Oregon's Outback*.

Both the Sheldon National Wildlife Refuge and the Hart Mountain National Antelope Refuge share some other similarities as well. For instance, both preserves were originally set aside to protect pronghorn, America's fastest land mammal. Both areas lie in the high desert region of the Great Basin, one of four North American deserts. And the two regions are administered by the U.S. Fish and Wildlife Service.

The refuge was originally set aside by Herbert Hoover in 1931. At that time, it consisted of just over 34,000 acres and was called the Charles Sheldon Wildlife Refuge. Five years later, Franklin D. Roosevelt created the Charles Sheldon Antelope Range and a whopping 540,000 acres received protection. In 1978, the two preserves joined together and the 575,000-acre preserve was renamed the Sheldon National Wildlife Refuge.

Obviously this northwestern Nevada countryside has changed dramatically since the days of pine forests and saber-toothed cats. Since then, volcanoes erupted, mountains emerged, growing along faults in the earth's crust, and glaciers and vast lakes covered much of the land, eventually carving the picture we see today.

As you drive through the refuge, you'll find the landscape is typical of that of the Great Basin region. With an elevation ranging from 4,500 to 7,600 feet above sea level (average is 6,000 feet), you'll find gentle hills, large tablelands that end abruptly in craggy rimrock cliffs, tight canyons that spill into rolling valleys. Sagebrush—both

Mountain lion.

big and low varieties—blankets much of the area along with a supply of rabbitbrush. Mountain mahogany, bitterbrush, and western juniper stands are found in the higher elevations above 6,000 feet. Spring-fed meadows, marshes, alkaline lakes, aspen-endowed canyons, and greasewood flats, add to the scene.

The refuge is a real treat for wildlife enthusiasts. Birders will thrill to 178 species of birds, best observed from May to October when there is the greatest diversity of bird life. As with any location, bird populations vary greatly according to the seasons. In the spring and fall, heavy migrations of waterbirds and waterfowl stop by for food and rest, with wetland areas providing food and cover for 80 percent of the wildlife species found on the refuge. There are at least 10 species of waterfowl nesting at the refuge, including mallards, teals, redheads, ruddy ducks, and Canada geese.

During the summer, a variety of birds of prey and various songbirds are present. Sage grouse concentrate in meadows during July and August, feeding on succulent wildflowers. Look for grouse in the evening hours at Hobble Spring and Cottonwood Meadows: Look for wildflowers sometime around the later part of May and beginning of June. Other bird life can be observed at Dufurrena Ponds, Catnip Reservoir and Big Springs Reservoir.

Pronghorn antelope baby approximately two days old.

A variety of mammals also inhabit the preserve with about 65 species calling it home for most of the year. There are 14 species of bats which migrate on a seasonal basis, opting to spend part of the year at another location. Other small creatures include porcupine, beaver, mice, squirrels, chipmunks, and rabbits.

Although many of the mammals are permanent inhabitants, they do move from place to place. For instance, as many as 3,500 pronghorn winter up on Big Spring Table, north of Duferrena Sub-headquarters. Moving south from Hart Mountain National Antelope Refuge, the animals are scattered throughout the area the rest of the year. The speedy mammals subsist on a diet of up to 90 percent sagebrush during the winter; bitterbrush is an important food source in late summer and fall.

If luck is on your side, you may see other large mammals in the form of coyote, mountain lion, deer, and California bighorn sheep. Although once abundant in northwestern Nevada, bighorn sheep disappeared from the area around 1930. A number of factors led to their demise—competition with domestic livestock, overhunting, and disease. California bighorn sheep have been re-established on the refuge, however. In 1968, the U.S. Fish and Wildlife Service transplanted eight sheep to an enclosure on Hell Creek. McGee Mountain was the site of a second reintroduction which took place in 1987. Although their numbers are still small in comparison to historic figures, the bighorn sheep population continues to grow.

Check with the refuge for the best sites for wildlife observation. I've been told that Swan Lake Reservoir is the best area for pronghorn during the summer months. Bighorn sheep usually gather for the rut (in October to November) in the vicinity of Hell Creek. They also inhabit McGee Mountain and the canyons south and east of the IXL Ranch. If you're looking for mule deer, try Badger Mountain.

Amphibians are limited in numbers with only three species found on the refuge. Usually too cold and dry to support much of a population, you can look for Pacific treefrogs, and Great Basin spadefoot toads, along stream courses, springs, ponds, and reservoirs. Bullfrogs, an introduced species, are found throughout Virgin Valley. Reptiles include seven species of lizards and seven species of snakes, including the western rat-tlesnake, which is found throughout the refuge. It is the only venomous reptile of which visitors should be aware.

Anglers may be tempted to head on over to the Sheldon for there are reports of excellent fishing conditions in good water years. You can cast a line in at several places on the refuge—Duferrena Ponds 20 and 21, Big Springs Reservoir, and McGee Pond. Please note, McGee Pond is open to a select group of people that includes all handicapped individuals, senior adults 65 and older, and children 12 and under. State regulations apply at all fishing areas.

Although limited by water availability, the area supports three species of native fish; tui chub, cutthroat trout, and Alvord chub. Refuge literature states "these native fishes are unique, as each population has adapted and evolved to its particular hot or cold spring, small creek, or lake."

Hiker at East Rim of Steens Mountain; Alvord Desert in back.

Bullfrog.

A variety of exotic (non-native) fish have been introduced for sport fishing. Dufurrena Ponds boast of largemouth bass, white crappie, pumpkinseed, bluegill, and yellow perch. Big Springs Reservoir offers rainbow trout in addition to cutthroat trout.

Hunting of mule deer, bighorn sheep, and pronghorn is allowed under Nevada Department of Wildlife regulations. In addition to big game, hunters vie for sage grouse, chukar, and California quail. All other wildlife (this includes reptiles, amphibians, birds, mammals, and even plants) are protected. Some areas are closed to hunting and are posted as such. Closed areas include the Hell Creek bighorn sheep enclosure, Duferrena, and Little Sheldon.

Whether you decide to spend part of the day or a week or more at the refuge, you'll find accommodations scarce. Camping is probably your best bet, especially if you're planning an extended visit. There's a hot springs and primitive campground (Virgin Valley) at the Duferrena

Sub-headquarters, and another hot springs north of State Highway 140 at Bog Hot Springs. There are a total of 19 primitive campsites, with several requiring a four-wheel drive or high clearance vehicle to gain access. Nine sites are accessible to passenger vehicles, however. These include Catnip Reservoir, West Rock Spring, Gooch Spring, Big Spring, Virgin Valley (mentioned previously), Horse Canyon Spring, Fish Spring, Badger, and Bateman Spring camps.

The Royal Peacock, a private campground, offers full hookups for a fee. It is located near two points of interest—the Virgin Valley Ranch, an historical site, and a patented mine offering opal hunting. There's a fee for mining.

Those opting for a motel will find the nearest facility at the Highway 140 junction, 2.4 miles south of Denio, which is 30 miles east of the Refuge Sub-headquarters at Dufurrena. There's also lodging and other necessities (gas and food) in Cedarville,

California, and Lakeview, Oregon. From sub-headquarters, it's about 70 miles southwest to Cedarville, approximately 90 miles northwest to Lakeview.

Whether camping or staying in a motel, most people seem to enjoy a nice, long soak in a hot springs. (As mentioned previously, there are two hot springs on the refuge available for public use.) Relics from the volcanic eruptions of the past, hot springs are a welcome treat, especially after a long, dusty drive, or a vigorous hike.

No doubt early man thought them just as refreshing. Archaeologists estimate that early man entered this area about 10,000 to 12,000 years ago, at a time when the lakes were receding. Here, as in areas of southeast Oregon, early man chipped away at various rock formations, drawing animals and symbols. Labeled petroglyphs (drawings carved into rocks), modern man has yet to determine the meaning of this unique art form.

About 1,500 years ago, the Shoshone and Northern Paiute Indians lived here. A nomadic people, they set up their wintering villages around warm springs. Eventually, the white man arrived and the Native Americans were herded to Indian Reservations while spacious cattle and sheep empires spread across the land.

Porcupine at Page Springs Campground.

Coyote.

Although the ranches prospered for a time, excessive use led to range deterioration, and serious problems for both the ranchers and native wildlife. Only a few small ranches remained on the Sheldon by the turn of the century, and efforts to save the area and its animal life prompted the designation of the refuge itself. If you have an interest in exploring and/or photographing historical sites, give Little Sheldon, Kinney Camp, Thousand Creek Ranch, and Last Chance Ranch, a try.

In addition to being of interest to history buffs, the refuge is a great place for those who like to engage in wildlife and plant observation, fishing, hunting, camping, hiking, and for those who make photographs. Those folks who are into rockhounding will also think of it as something special. Please note, there's a seven pound limit per person per day on the refuge. An exception to this rule lies within the Virgin Valley Mining District. According to refuge personnel, "Within the district there are thousands of mine claims, some of which are patented. Permission from claim owners must be obtained for rock collecting."

Established for the mining of Virgin Valley Fire Opals, Nevada's state gemstone, the Virgin Valley Mining District covers 67,000 acres of refuge lands. Although you won't be allowed to mine for the rare gems on the majority of claims, there are two patented mines—Rainbow Ridge and Royal Peacock—that offer opal hunting for a fee.

As you explore the refuge, you'll find it's one huge, expansive place, an isolated region where help may be hours away should you have some sort of problem. Inquire at Refuge Headquarters in Lakeview, Oregon, or Refuge Sub-headquarters at Dufurrena, for current updates regarding road conditions. This warning is especially necessary in the winter and spring when road conditions vary more than usual. Except for paved State Highway 140, all roads are either gravel county roads or jeep trails. Some of the jeep trails are very rough and require both a high clearance vehicle and four-wheel drive.

Refuge personnel encourage all visitors to carry extra gasoline, water, tires, and a First-Aid kit. If visiting in the summer, be sure to pack extra drinking water, sunblock, and insect repellent.

Weather is typical of the Great Basin desert which means you should plan on hot summers and cold winters. (Special note: Most of the refuge is inaccessible in the winter.)

For additional information contact the Sheldon National Wildlife Refuge. (See page 86 for address.)

Mule Deer in the Malheur National Wildlife Refuge.

Steens Mountain & Alvord Valley

Recently I was able to fly over the Steens Mountain/Alvord Valley area. Fascinated by what lay beneath my feet—the jagged, serrated gorges of the Steens east side, the vastness of the Alvord Desert—I listened as a fellow passenger, also wide-eyed and astonished at the scene before him, remarked to no one in particular. "You know," he said, "you couldn't have one without the other. Those two—the Steens and the Alvord—are definitely related."

Steens Mountain was "born" approximately 15 million years ago when a fracture developed along what is now the eastern base. Repeated uplifting pushed the fault up, tilting the surface of the block gently to the west and exposing the layers of underlying formations on the east side. Although the crest of the fault block is currently 5,500 feet (more than a mile) above the Alvord Valley (sometimes called the Alvord Basin), it was even higher before erosion took its toll. Ravaged by the effects of erosion—glacial activity, rain, and wind—this mountain is more weather-worn than other southeast Oregon scarps. Geologists blame altitude and a steeper gradient as the main reasons for the extended wear.

Steens Mountain is known as a "fault block" mountain by geologists. Like others of its kind, it is distinguished by one face which is almost perpendicular, whereas the other face climbs at a sluggish pace for many miles. With the fault facing east, it's a hasty three miles from the 9,773-foot summit to the desert floor more than a mile below. Although the average slope of the eastern scarp measures 20 degrees, the western slopes average a mere three degrees. To put this into perspective, if you head up the mountain from the west you'd travel 23 miles to get from base level— about 4,000 feet—to the summit.

Although this geological event took place a long time ago, today's visitors see the results of that sinking. And if you're like most visitors, you'll stand in awe of the wondrous spectacle before you.

To those who frequent the region described in this guidebook, Steens Mountain is a well-known destination, a land of wind and wildflowers, of quaking aspens singing in the summer and glowing a golden farewell come fall. It's a land rich in contrast with fascinating glacier-carved gorges awaiting anxious hikers and horsemen. It's a place where wild horses roam at will, a land where wide vistas are free for the asking, a place where visitors can just sit and ponder.

The Alvord Valley is just as inspiring with its alkali lakes, its hot springs, its unique plant and animal life, its ghost towns, and its inspiring, spiritual view of Steens Mountain. The valley extends for seventy miles in a mostly north-south direction, its arid plains paralleling both the Steens and Pueblo Mountains.

With an annual precipitation of seven inches or less, it's no wonder most people are completely taken by surprise upon spying several lakes which shimmer in Oregon's truest desert. From 1898 to 1912 Borax Lake was harvested for—as you may have guessed—borax. Located seven miles north-northeast of Fields, the Rose Valley Borax Company collected and processed the alkali crust circling the lake, and the resultant product (400 tons of crystallized borax) was shipped by 16-mule team to the railroad at Winnemucca, 130 miles south. When deposits were found closer to the rails, the mine closed down. The remains of two large vats are still visible, as are traces of a sod house, which provided shelter for the Chinese laborers.

Travel another two miles north of Borax Lake and you'll find Alvord Lake with

Like the Alvord Valley, Steens Mountain is comprised of one magical ecological delight after another. With a base elevation of 4,000 feet or so, visitors climb through eight vegetative zones—ranging from the arid sagebrush region to the snowcover zone or alpine tundra—en route to the 9,773-foot summit, the highest in southeast Oregon.

Enter the world of Steens Mountain in the sagebrush belt where scattered areas of western juniper grow amid both big and low sagebrush. Definitely the most common

Kiger Gorge, Steens Mountain.

its long band of sand dunes paralleling its east side. The computer disk-flat Alvord Desert lies north of the lake, a smooth playa of sand and dust. In wet years, the basin fills with water which later evaporates.

shrub on the mountain, sagebrush varies in size according to elevation and wind conditions. Next, you'll pass through areas of western juniper and mountain mahogany before emerging into the mountain big sagebrush zone. Wildflowers grow in abundance in this area, with the Steens Mountain thistle (an endemic species growing only on Steens Mountain) observed along the roadside in many places within this zone.

The quaking aspen vegetative zone wanders between 6,000 and 8,000 feet and is particularly impressive. Here, elegant groves of aspens lure photographers and other visitors who come every fall to capture the mesmerizing yellow and gold image. Next comes the subalpine meadow zone and the subalpine grassland belt which harbors the endemic Steens Mountain paintbrush.

Wildflower enthusiasts may have a difficult time determining the best time to visit for the colorful blossoms grace the mountain slopes at various times of the year. Depending on the elevation and exposure to sun or shade, species such as white wyethia, blue camas, clarkia, and wild phlox may decorate the sage-blessed lower slopes during the late spring—April through June is usually good for areas below 6,000 feet— while the upper mountain may be blanketed by snow. Visit the upper zones in late August, however, and alpine blossoms will surely decorate the scene.

Although the grassland zone is mostly barren today, there was a time when native bunchgrasses spread across the lofty slopes. Unfortunately, excessive grazing (early in the twentieth century as many as 180,000 sheep foraged these slopes during the summer) denuded the slopes, exposing bare soil. Today, sheep still graze on parts of the western slopes of the Steens.

But all that could change in the near future as major transformations are in the air. And like all changes—both good and bad—there are those who welcome them and those who oppose them.

Amid proposals of a 500,000-acre Steens Mountain National Park and a 523,000-acre Steens Mountain National Preserve, there are cattle ranchers who rigidly detest the plan, their grazing rights threatened. With mining rights and geothermal activity threatened as well, the debate continues to heat up. If managed by the National Park Service, grazing and mining appropriations would be null and void.

Bill Marlett of the Oregon Natural Desert Association, a grass-roots conservation group working with other environmental groups to preserve the state's high desert heritage, insists on protecting Steens Mountain and other desert areas against cattle which annihilate native vegetation and the habitat of dependent wildlife. If conservationists win the ongoing battle, ONDA claims "a Steens National Park and Preserve would restore and enhance the wild character of the Steens for present and future generations." Although hunting would be banned in the park itself, it would be allowed in the preserve.

Some argue that park designation will bring increased tourism, traffic that will somehow harm the land. True, visitor use will increase, but it's evident that thousands of visitors are already "discovering" Steens Mountain. Bureau of Land Management (BLM), managing agency for the area, estimates that 48,000 people visit Steens Mountain every year. Increased use is probably inevitable, but park studies show most visitors use only two percent of park lands. Step out of your car, walk a short distance, and you'll usually have the place to yourself.

Although National Park and Preserve status may take some time, a wilderness study program on Steens Mountain is currently in effect. Although there are no designated wilderness areas on the mountain, visitors will encounter five—High Steens, South Fork Donner und Blitzen River, Blitzen River, Little Blitzen Gorge, and Bridge Creek—Wilderness Study Areas. These are sections of land currently under review for possible inclusion in the National Wilderness Preservation System designated as such by Congress. Administered by the BLM, the total study area is comprised of 187,120 acres.

Still, all controversy aside, the mountain is a potpourri of ecological wonders. More than 600 species of plants adorn its slopes and gorges, its waterways and ponds. In addition, there are more than 250

Horse at Riddle Brothers Ranch, Steens Mountain.

species of amphibians, reptiles, birds, and mammals inhabiting the area.

Various forms of animal life tiptoe through gorges and canyons, grace the mountain slopes and valleys, flit from tree to tree and bush to bush along riparian streams, and nest among rimrock cliffs. Beavers are in evidence along almost every stream on the mountain's west side; golden eagles and a variety of other raptors soar in the endless skies; owls silently patrol the star-studded night sky. Bighorn sheep scramble up and down the rocky, nearly vertical east face, while pronghorn, mule deer, and an occasional Rocky Mountain elk forage on the grassy western slopes.

Although the Alvord Valley may seem empty and void of animal life to some, if you look closely and explore at the proper time, you may see pronghorn, bighorn sheep, and mule deer. Smaller mammals include the badger, marmot, wood rat or pack rat, kit fox, coyote, porcupine, rabbit and jackrabbit, and perhaps the most common animal, the kangaroo rat. And Borax Lake is home to the endangered Borax Lake chub.

Riddle Brothers Ranch, Steens Mountain.

Various raptors—bald and golden eagles, northern harriers, American kestrels, red-tailed hawks—ply the endless skies. A variety of birds nest here as well, with killdeer, magpie, common raven, and Brewer's blackbird raising their offspring in the area. A number of reptiles and amphibians also call the Alvord home. These include the whipsnake, garter snake, and rattlesnake. Amphibians are few, but they include the western toad, Pacific tree toad, spotted frog, and western spadefoot frog.

Dwelling in the glacier-carved lakes of the Steens, anglers try for the endemic Lahontan cutthroat trout in Wildhorse Lake; they catch rainbow and brook trout in Fish Lake; they hook native redband trout in both Fish Lake and the Donner und Blitzen National Wild and Scenic River; and some of the desert lakes such as Mann Lake provide for great fishing as well, with Lahontan cutthroat and rainbow trout particular favorites.

Steens Mountain is also home to the Kiger mustang, thought to be one of the purest wild herds of Spanish mustangs in the world. Horse enthusiasts and wild horse authorities alike agree "no other horse in America is quite like the Kiger Mustang found on Steens Mountain." Although most folks will not be able to recognize the difference between a Kiger mustang and the free-roaming wild horses which number about 300 and also live on Steens Mountain, the Kiger mustang possesses all of the characteristics of the Spanish Barb from which the Spanish Mustang descended. In direct comparison, the wild horse is usually a mixed breed. (For the record, the South Steens wild horse herd descended from a number of renegade horses that escaped from a variety of sources—Indians, ranchers, early explorers, settlers, and miners.)

Noted for their stamina and intelligence, Kiger mustangs are slightly smaller than modern-day horses, with small, round bones, and small feet. With a fine muzzle and distinctly hooked ear tips, the mustang also has prominent, wide set eyes.

At one time the mustang, the horse that helped settle the west, was thought to be extinct. Today, BLM manages the Kiger mustang under the Wild Free-Roaming Horse and Burro Act. According to BLM, "Two areas have been set aside to reduce the chance of losing all of the animals, should a natural catastrophe occur. These areas are known as the Kiger and the Riddle Mountain Herd Management Areas (HMA)." The Kiger HMA consists of nearly 37,000 acres and anywhere from 51 to 82 horses. The Riddle Mountain HMA supports from 33 to 56 horses ranging over nearly 29,000 acres. Some of the horses are transferred from group to group periodically to prevent inbreeding.

When the population of both the Kiger mustangs and the wild horses reach the maximum number, the excess is rounded up and shipped over to the Burns District Wild Horse Corrals where they are made available for adoption. For more information about the BLM's Adopt-A-Horse Program, contact their Hines office listed on page 86.

Unlike many Oregon peaks, Steens Mountain is accessible to everyone. Drive to a point near the East Rim via Oregon's highest road, and you can walk a hundred feet or so to the edge and gaze down more than one mile to the vast Alvord Basin below. Admire the scene all around you and you'll see portions of four states—California, Nevada, Idaho and Oregon. It's a sight you won't soon forget.

Steens Mountain was named after Major Enoch Steen of the 1st U.S. Dragoons. (For those who might expect the correct term to be Steen's Mountain, the accepted name is Steens.) Major Steen was ordered to the area in 1860 to check out the possibility of routes linking the Willamette Valley to southeastern Oregon. Along the way he encountered a band of Paiute Indians and chased them up the Donner und Blitzen River drainage, over Steens Mountain, and down rugged Wildhorse Canyon to the Alvord Desert. Obsessed with their capture, he continued to chase them south into Nevada, but called off the chase when he lost track of the Paiutes near Disaster Peak.

Although Major Steens and his men hardly had time to sit and enjoy the scene, today's visitors consist of a vast assortment of people, some of whom come just for that purpose—to sit and gaze to their heart's content. Others come to explore. While the majority of summer visitors come to hike, photograph, and sightsee, the region is also popular with upland game bird hunters who yearn for sage grouse, quail, and chukar. Big game hunters also stalk deer, antelope, and bighorn sheep (by special permit only). Fishing is favored as well, with scenic Fish Lake decorating the western slope of the

Steens Mountain at first light as seen from Alvord Desert.

mountain, while providing a favorite place for both anglers and campers.

As you travel along Steens Mountain, you may come to think of it as an island of sorts. Standing alone in all its glory, the rim averages 9,300 feet in elevation and spans a distance of about 30 miles. Surrounded by high desert, the mountain has a climate all its own, especially near the summit where the weather can vary greatly from that of the areas encircling it.

Glacial evidence is obvious when viewing any of the magnificent U-shaped gorges that gouge this mountain, but there's a nearly picture-perfect example at Kiger Gorge. From this viewpoint, the land just drops away before you, swept into a vast bowl of cliffs and canyon polished by the ravages of mighty glacial rivers which swept through the area eons ago.

Whereas you can see the gorges and much of Steens Mountain from the comfort of your motor vehicle, hiking the back-country is perhaps the best way to really see the area. Although you won't find much in the way of maintained trails, you will find numerous animal tracks to explore, and it's often fun to take off, topographic map in hand, and bushwhack to some unknown point.

Day hikers and backpackers will want to check

out the Desert Trail, part of the Oregon State Recreational Trail System. Although far from complete, the trail passes through the Steens area, leading north from the Alvord Desert, up over the mountain, and on to the Page Springs Campground and points north. The proposed route will extend roughly 1,800 to 2,000 miles from Mexico to Canada, traversing the mostly arid lands east of the Sierra Nevada and Cascade Mountain ranges. When completed, it will become a part of the National Desert Trail. Although the trail is not (nor are there plans for it to be) a constructed path, a clearly defined trail, "it is perceived as a corridor without specific borders, through which the hiker may pass choosing his/her own route." Intermittent rock cairns indicate the general direction of the trail and high quality maps are available for portions of the route. These topographic field guides provide specific route information, hiking tips, and much more.

Maps are available from the Desert Trail Association, P.O. Box 537, Burns, OR 97720. They welcome new members and urge everyone to become a part of this national conservation-recreation oriented organization dedicated to the development of the National Desert Scenic Trail and the protection of the Western Desert.

The best access to Steens Mountain is via the 66-mile Steens Mountain National Back Country Byway, which encompasses 52-mile Steens Mountain Loop Road, a graded gravel road which is very rough in spots. Summer and early fall are the best times for traveling the route, although portions of it are usually open by late spring. For specific road and route information, see the Steens Mountain Loop tour.

A number of dirt roads lead off the main path to some interesting old cabins, the homes of early settlers such as the Riddle Brothers, and other hearty souls who struggled upon the land, fighting to keep food on the table. And then there's Whorehouse Meadow, a forest of quaking aspens upon which bored Basque sheepherders carved their most explicit fantasies.

Those searching for the Riddle Brothers Ranch will have to check with the BLM regarding its accessibility. The ranch is currently under a reconstruction phase and is not yet open to the public. Upon opening, however, the BLM will provide for interpretation and a trail along the Little Blitzen River will lead to the ranch and many historic exhibits.

Walter, Frederick, and Benjamin Riddle, three bachelor brothers, secured homesites and grazed livestock on more than 1,000 acres of Steens Mountain land. According to the BLM, "The Riddle Brothers Ranch was part of Oregon's last frontier, the settlement on semiarid lands which intensified speculation and homesteading in the northern Great Basin between 1900 and 1920. The ranch is a uniquely preserved ensemble of buildings which give testimony to livestock raising and lifestyle 'out back of beyond'."

Several campgrounds adjoin the byway, making this loop a real treat for those with a tent or RV, or for those who only need to throw down their bag under the diamond-studded sky. If comfortable lodging (ie. a warm bed, hot shower) is more to your liking, then you'll want to check out the famous Frenchglen Hotel at 503-493-2825. Located at the starting point for the Steens Mountain Loop Tour, this small historic hotel offers eight rooms and family dining at large communal tables.

With a weather pattern all its own, you should be prepared for extreme conditions anytime of the year atop Steens Mountain. Watch for lightning storms, high winds, snow, and rain year-round. Summer daytime temperatures normally range in the 70 to 80s, with an occasional high in the 90s. Nighttime temperatures may dip down to the mid-teens and low 20s. The roadway is usually closed by heavy snow from November through June.

The Alvord Valley is accessible year-round. See Alvord Desert Tour for additional information.

If you need more information, including up-to-date news regarding road openings and closures, et cetera, write or call BLM, Burns District Office. (See page 86 for address.)

The
Owyhee
River.

Auto Tours

Wagontire

Frenchglen

Lakeview

Fields

Vale

Plush

BURNS

ROME

Adel

Denio

Lawen

Hines

Fish Lake

of Oregon's Outback

Introduction to Auto Tour Guide

Although the following auto tour guides have been designed with the utmost care, they are not, as the old cliche goes, carved in stone. In fact, they were written with change in mind. After venturing over to southeast Oregon on many occasions over the past few years, I've found out what works best for me. But that's me. If you'd rather explore just a portion of one of the tours, then by all means do so. If traveling the tour in the opposite direction from which I've written suits you better, then go for it. And if you'd prefer combining two of the tours and making it a longer visit, then you should do that too. The decision is up to you.

Before I explain how to use the auto tour portion of this guidebook, I must give you two words of advice. I think it's good advice and if you follow it closely you're bound to have a lot more fun. My tip for the day? When exploring southeast Oregon, try to "wing it" as much as possible. If you're heading from one site to the next and something exciting happens (let's say an enormous bighorn ram crosses the road in front of you), stop. Spend time watching the awesome creature before you. If you don't make it to the spot you were headed to that day, you can always visit the site the next day.

I've found that winging it is the best attitude for driving remote roads, too. While you should carry a good supply of water, warm clothing, some spare automobile parts, and of course, a spare tire, remember, if something goes wrong, the nearest town and tow truck may be miles and miles away. Visit the region knowing that you're exploring a remote area, an intriguing place of solitude, abundant animal life, and so on, and if you break down or something, perhaps it won't be so bad.

Winging it also helps in terms of exploring. One of the best things about getting out in the boondocks is the opportunity to be adventurous. If you're traveling along and you see a road or path heading off to some unknown point, why not drive down the road or walk the path and see what's there. Grab your day pack, fill it with a few snacks, some water, a First-aid kit, perhaps a sweater or jacket, a compass, and a topographic map, and you're all set for a little adventure.

I guess winging it boils down to making the time to slow down and enjoy the scenery, the wildlife, the isolation of a place I call "Oregon's Outback." It's leaving the wristwatch at home. It's getting away from a schedule which says you have to be here and there at a certain time. It's having fun and enjoying this magnificent land.

I've divided southeast Oregon into six different auto tour trips. Some are Loop Tours, others are one-way affairs. There are also a number of tour connectors that provide the mileage and insight into what to see and do when linking one trip with another. Information regarding things to see and do along the way are included in the mileage logs, as well, with the amenities for each town listed.

Remember, many of these towns are the close-your-eyes-and-sneeze-and-you'll-miss-it-type towns. When available, motel and campground accommodations are mentioned for

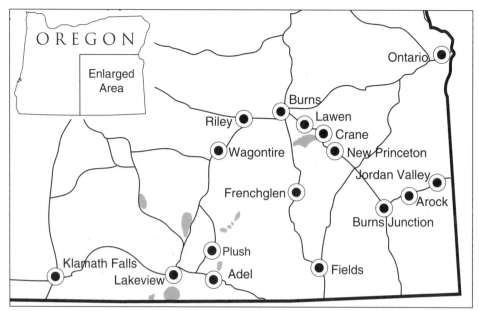

each town. Also, campgrounds along the route are pinpointed for your convenience. Restaurants, markets, and gas stations also receive recognition.

In regards to distances from point to point, place to place, I've noted both the mileage from Point A to Point B and the running total for each trip is noted in parentheses. When driving the Hart Mountain Tour, for example, you would read the following:

0.0   0.0)   From Lakeview, head north on U.S. 395 and State Highway 140 East, both of which are paved.

4.7   (4.7)   Exit U.S. 395, now driving east on State Highway 140 through the Warner Mountains, past the Warner Canyon Ski Area. Located at the 5,846-foot level, the area offers both downhill and cross-country skiing.

15.5   (20.2)   Turn left (north) onto paved Lake 3-13 County Road, traveling toward Plush and Hart Mountain. You'll cross an enormous nearly-flat plateau blanketed with sagebrush and other high desert vegetation before dropping down through a rocky pass to the tiny town of Plush.

As you can see, the total mileage from Lakeview to Plush is 20.2 miles. If you'd rather count the miles from place to place, however, then you have that option. For instance, it is 15.5 miles from the turnoff on U.S. 395 to Plush.

Reference has been made to road conditions as well. I've specified which roads are paved, which are gravel, and which ones are dirt. I've also made note of the roads where a high clearance or four-wheel drive vehicle is recommended. If certain roads are closed during specific times of the year, I've also jotted that information down for your convenience.

Hiking trails and side trips are easy to find as they are printed in boldface type. Although I've mentioned some hiking trails and side trips, I would definitely recommend taking off from any point of your own choosing and exploring on your own. I think you'll find it really is the best way to get a good feel for this magnificent country.

One more important note. There's a list of addresses and phone numbers on page 86 of this guide that will be most helpful for those in need of more information regarding the places I've written about.

Happy traveling!

Hart Mountain Tour

Although it's certainly possible to drive this 110-mile (not including the side trips) tour in one day, I'd recommend spending at least two days doing so, more if you're interested in exploring much of the Hart Mountain National Antelope Refuge.

The fun begins in Lakeview, a livestock, agricultural, and timber town, settled in 1889. Although you can't see the lake from town, Lakeview was named for its nearby acquaintance, Goose Lake.

The town is situated at the base of the Warner Mountains, and is known as the "tallest" incorporated town in the Beaver State. At an elevation of 4,800 feet, the town seems proud to be the tallest, with signs boasting of the fact. Lanky wooden cowboys, tall hats and all, greet those entering the town. But Lakeview is more than just the tallest town, it's also been officially titled the "Hang Gliding Capital of the West."

Hang gliders flock to the area during the Fourth of July weekend when several hundred people glide in to take advantage of the area's rolling hills and flat land—perfect terrain for take-offs and landings.

Lakeview visitors will find plenty in the way of amenities, with a variety of restaurants and motels to suit all needs. Also, there are a number of campgrounds in and near town.

The Lake County Museum is probably the best way to get a feel for the area. There are more than 1,000 museum pieces ranging from a piece of petrified wood thought to be 110-120 million years old, to a pair of bark and plant sandals, carbon dated at 9,000 years old. The museum is open seasonally, from mid-May to the end of September. Another must-see is the Schminck Museum, located on E Street next to the county museum. It depicts the history of one family, while the county museum is a historical collection of important events and people.

If hiking is your pleasure, then you'll want to explore the Crane Mountain Recreation Trail. Located in the Fremont National Forest, east of Lakeview, there are full directions to the trailhead at the end of this chapter.

Golfers can swing at a nine-hole course located three miles south of town. Said to be one of the most difficult in the state for its size, there are numerous sand traps and a pond.

A popular geological attraction includes Old Perpetual Geyser, Oregon's only continuously spouting geyser. Visible as you head north out of town, the geyser erupts every 90 seconds and shoots 60 feet into the air. Hunter's Hot Springs is home for the geyser, an oasis of hot springs and wildlife. Located on 47 acres, there are numerous hot springs pools and ponds, a fresh water jacuzzi, a restaurant, and bed and breakfast accommodations.

From Lakeview, you'll head northeast through the Great Basin Desert to the tiny town of Plush. If you're interested in gems and fine jewelry, be sure to stop in at the jewelry store where Wayne Hartgraves and his son, David Hohman, create unique, handmade pieces. If

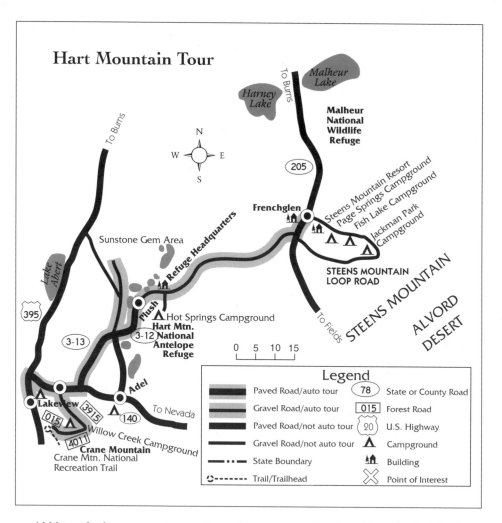

you'd like to find some sunstones, Oregon's state gem, there's a side trip which leads to the Sunstone Gemstone area.

From Plush, the trip to Hart Mountain National Antelope Refuge is one of great beauty as you pass through the Warner Valley and a series of shallow lakes, also known as potholes. A wall of rugged cliffs looms to the east along the western edge of Hart Mountain, a striking fault-block mountain. Home for bighorn sheep, from atop the expansive plateau at Hart Mountain, you can look for pronghorn, camp among the aspens, explore one of many canyons, and hike to the top of Warner Peak.

The trip ends at Frenchglen, a don't-blink-or-you'll-miss-it town that's also an historic site. It's the jumping off point for the Steens Mountain Loop Tour as well.

Mileage Log

0.0   (0.0) From Lakeview, head north on U.S. 395 and State Highway 140 East, both of which are paved.

4.7   (4.7) Exit U.S. 395, now driving east on State Highway 140 through the Warner Mountains, past the Warner Canyon Ski Area. Located at the 5,846-foot level, the area offers both downhill and cross-country skiing.

15.5 (20.2) Turn left (north) onto paved Lake 3-13 County Road, traveling toward Plush and Hart Mountain. You'll cross an enormous nearly-flat plateau blanketed with sagebrush and other high desert vegetation before dropping down through a rocky pass to the tiny town of Plush.

18.5 (38.7) Plush, an old ranching community, once bragged of a population of 2,000 back in the 1920s. Today there is a combination gas and grocery store, a rest area with toilets and a picnic area. Be sure to visit Plush "Diamond" Works, P.O. Box 50, Plush, OR 97637; (503) 947-3194. (For more information, see side trip to Sunstone Gemstone Area.)

0.8 (39.5) Just north of town, turn east on Lake 3-12 County Road. As you head out of town, you'll pass Hart Lake and the Warner Wetlands Area of Critical Environmental Concern. Later, the paved road parallels the rugged west slope of Hart Mountain.

6.6 46.1) Enter Hart Mountain National Antelope Refuge. Drive another mile and the road turns into a well-maintained gravel road. Now's your chance to scan the nearby cliffs for bighorn sheep. Hart Mountain was home to the bighorns long before America was settled. In fact, Indian drawings show figures of wild sheep, an indication of their importance to these first inhabitants. Unfortunately, the westward migration brought overanxious hunters and domestic sheep, and the bighorns disappeared in the early 1900s.

Help was on the way, however, when the Oregon State Commission joined forces with the U.S. Fish and Wildlife Service in transporting 20 California Bighorn Sheep (*Ovis canadensis californiana*) from B.C. Canada in 1954. The effort was a success, thus the 450 sheep living there today.

You'll drive parallel to the mountain for a while, then the road winds up and over the range providing a wonderful view west to the Warner Potholes.

16.3 (62.4) Hart Mountain National Antelope Refuge Headquarters. You'll find water, a restroom, and if you need any other information there are usually park personnel around the area. Jackrabbits are usually seen in large numbers come early morning and late evening.

Those in search of a campsite or just a place to explore, should head south toward the aspen-decorated Hot Springs Campground. You'll reach a junction in 1.7 miles; head right 2.3 miles to the campground where there are toilets and a hot springs which is enclosed for privacy; other services are nonexistent.

If you'd like a good overall view of the refuge, especially the area to the west, head left at the junction, traveling 4.0 miles to signed Lookout Point. This road is open from November 1 through May 25.

To continue on to Frenchglen, drive east while traveling across a vast sagebrush plateau, passing Rock Creek Reservoir, en route.

40.7 (103.1) Reach paved State Highway 205. Make a left, passing an occasional ranch as you descend to the 4,200-foot mark at Frenchglen.

6.7 (109.8) Frenchglen is a tiny hamlet set among an oasis of tall shade trees, a place where one can sit and while away the day drinking ice tea. Named for Peter French and his father-in-law, Dr. Hugh Glenn, it is located about 60 miles south of Burns. The town offers a combination market/post office/gas station, a one-room schoolhouse, and the Frenchglen Hotel, listed on the National Registry of Historic Places.

The hotel, which was built in 1924, is open March 1 through November 15. An Oregon State Wayside, the eight-room hotel is usually filled to capacity; reservations are recommended. If you enjoy good food, stop by for a meal. The family style meals are served three times daily. Although you needn't be a guest at the hotel to enjoy the dinner, reservations are a must.

Side Trip To Sunstone Gem Area

Plush diamonds (Oregon sunstones) are easily found about 25 miles north of Plush in the 2,560-acre Mineral Withdrawal Area. Maintained by the BLM, the stones are a semi-precious mineral feldspar, most of which are clear or yellowish in color. The rarest forms are lavender; blue and canary colored stones are almost as rare.

Although the stones are easily found on the surface of the ground, I'm told the deeper you go, the more rare the colors you will find. Early morning and afternoon are the best times for spotting the stones as the sunlight is more likely to "spotlight" your quarry.

For a fine look at Plush diamonds, be sure to stop by Plush 'Diamond' Works, located in downtown Plush. Wayne Hartgraves, owner of the shop, showcases his work, turning a rough gem into an exquisite piece of jewelry.

To reach the Sunstone area from Plush, head north toward Hart Mountain National Antelope Refuge, remaining on a BLM Road instead of turning east on Lake County 3-12 toward Hart Mountain. Follow the signs to the Sunstone Gem Area.

Side Trip To Crane Mountain

Crane Mountain Trail begins at Willow Creek Campground and extends past Crane Mountain to the California border. Although a truly impressive hike, I've included a short, two-mile round-trip section of the hike which puts one atop Crane Mountain in a jiffy. For those interested in a topographic map of the area, use the Crane Mountain USGS quad.

The trail grade is easy to moderate, with the elevation fluctuating between 8,240 and 8,456 feet. While the views are outstanding, so are the opportunities to observe wildlife and wildflowers. Mid-June through early November is the best time to visit.

To reach the trailhead from downtown Lakeview, drive north on U.S. 395/Oregon 140 for 4.7 miles. At this point, State Highway 140 East branches off to the right. Follow it 7.1 miles to S. Warner Rd. (Forest Road 3915) an asphalt road which turns to gravel in a few miles. After traveling 10.1 miles on Forest Road 3915, turn right on Forest Road 4011. In less than a mile you'll pass the turnoff (Forest Road 011) to the Willow Creek Campground. You'll find picnic tables, fire pits, outhouses, and water, at the free camp.

After traveling a total of 3.6 miles on Forest Road 4011, the road changes to Forest Road 015, a narrow, rocky, dirt road. Those with low clearance vehicles will have to park here and walk to the trailhead which is another 2.6 miles beyond. En route to the trailhead, you'll see a dirt road taking off to the right. Follow this a short distance for a wonderful view from 7,515-foot Willow Point.

Before jumping out at the trailhead, you'll want to continue up the road another 0.2 mile to the site of an old lookout. From here there are terrific views of the Warner Mountains, Steens Mountain, and beyond. You'll see into four states—Oregon, California, Idaho and Nevada.

From the trailhead, head south on the Crane Mountain National Recreation Trail, hiking nearly level ground for 0.8 mile. Once the trail begins descending, look for orange flagging on the right. Flagging leads to Crane Mountain's highest point, approximately 0.2 mile to the west. Views are breathtaking from the ridge.

Those desiring a longer hike can continue along the Crane Mountain Trail which stretches a total of 8.7 miles from the site of the old lookout south into California. Along the way look for bighorn sheep, mule deer, coyotes, and other mammals.

For more information contact Lakeview Ranger District, address and phone on page 86.

Steens Mountain Loop Tour

T he 66-mile Steens Mountain Loop Tour is a definite must-see for I can't think of another drive in this part of the country that comes even close to it in magnificence, sheer beauty, and that kind of awe-inspiring feeling one gets when they know they've latched onto something special.

The trip promises a potpourri of natural delights ranging from glacier-carved gorges and endless views to wild horses and dancing wildflowers to ribbons of aspens and solitude.

Aspens. They inspire the soul whether stark naked in the winter, fully clothed during the summer, or dressed in reds and golds in the fall.

Wildflowers. A rainbow of delicate jewels grace the nearly barren slopes in the summer.

Kiger Mustangs. Steeds roam at will.

Panoramas. Seemingly endless views prompt visitors to stand and gaze upon the majesty of Steens Mountain.

The fun begins at Frenchglen, an old ranching community about 60 miles south of Burns. From town, you'll climb up the west side of the mountain, sliding past a number of scenic lakes and Kiger Gorge, to the summit, the highest peak in southeast Oregon. Although a lot of folks will be happy with the wide views visible from their automobiles, I'd encourage you to get out, to explore some of the gorges, to drink in the wildness and richness of Steens Mountain.

You'll travel via a gravel road (sometimes rough) for most of the loop. The best time for travel is late spring, summer, and fall. Although the lower gates typically open sometime around the first of May, heavy snow usually keeps the upper gates closed until mid-July.

Mileage Log

0.0 (0.0) From Frenchglen, a picturesque town resting among a lush oasis of lofty trees, and site of the historic Frenchglen Hotel (see the Hart Mountain Tour for more information), head east on Steens Mountain Loop Road. The gravel road skirts the southern portion of Malheur National Wildlife Refuge. (For information on the refuge see the Malheur National Wildlife Refuge Tour.)

1.5 (1.5) P Ranch Headquarters. This is a good place to look for turkey vultures and other bird life.

1.5 (3.0) Steens Mountain Resort is a private campground near the Donner und Blitzen River. Situated atop a small hillside where there is a good view of the area, the resort offers 97 sites for tents or trailers, full hook-ups (water, electricity, sewer), satellite television, laundry and shower facilities, and a store.

Hiking Trail: This is also a jumping-off point for the Desert Trail. The trail consists of an old jeep road and follows the east fence line for about five miles. The trailhead is located between the West Canal and the cattle guard at the entrance to the Steens Mountain Resort. (For more information on the Desert Trail see the Steens Mountain & Alvord Valley chapter.)

Steens Mountain Loop Tour

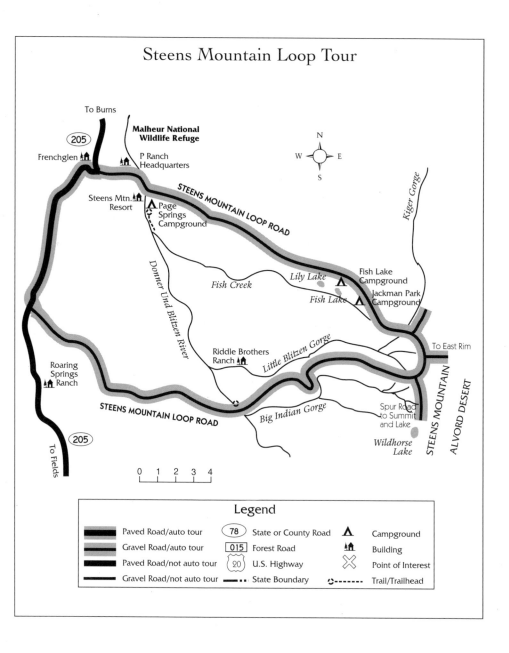

0.1 (3.1) Turnoff for Page Springs Campground. It's only 0.3 mile to the BLM facility, located along the Donner und Blitzen River. There are 30 sites (with picnic tables and fire grates), toilets, and water. The fee is $3. It's half that price for seniors with a Golden Age passport and handicapped individuals with a Golden Access passport. Horses are not allowed.

From the campground entrance, continue up the Steens Mountain Loop Road. Although the road up the mountain is newly graded, only small RVs should consider making the trip because the south half is sometimes rough.

Donner und Blitzen River near Page Springs Campground.

Hiking Trails: If you enjoy hiking, there are a couple of good family hikes accessible from the campground. The first is a signed Nature Trail, located across from Campsite 15. The trail is steep, climbing 0.2 mile to the top of a ridge where rock outcrops provide a good vantage point. You'll see north and west to the Blitzen Valley, Frenchglen, and the Malheur National Wildlife Refuge. There's another trail at the far end of the campground. Closed to motorized vehicles, numerous trails parallel the river, where rim-rock-lined canyons narrow as you travel south. Bald eagles call the upper reaches of the Blitzen River Canyon home in the winter and spring.

12.2 (15.3) Lily Lake, home to boreal toads and Pacific treefrogs. There's a primitive campsite at the water lily-blessed lake. A picnic table is the only amenity.

  1.3 (16.6) Fish Lake and Campground—elevation 7,371 feet. Facilities include 20 sites (with picnic tables and fire grates), water, and toilets. Fees are the same as those at Page Springs Campground. Fishing is popular at the moraine lake which is ringed with aspens year-round. Wildflowers add to the scene in the proper season.

  0.3 (16.9) Pate Lake; picnic tables and fire pits.

1.9 (18.8) Jackman Park Campground. There's water and toilets at this small six-site campground.

3.9 (22.7) Kiger Gorge turnoff on the left. This is a definite must-see! A spur road leads to a viewpoint, 0.4 mile away. Definitely one of the most spectacular spots on the Steens, the U-shaped cirque is textbook-perfect. For a totally different view, some folks hike into the gorge via game trails.

As you continue up to the East Rim, you'll pass Little Blitzen Gorge. Notice how glaciers nearly cut through the mountain at this point.

2.8 (25.5) Junction to the East Rim and Steens Summit. Make a left, staying on the road as you drive another 0.4 mile to a parking area. It's a short walk to the edge of the rim (elevation 9,730 feet) for a splendid view of the Alvord Desert and Basin, and points beyond. If you're interested in standing atop the true summit, head back to the junction where you'll take the middle road to Steens Summit and the Wildhorse Lake viewpoint. A dirt road leads 2.0 miles to a closed gate. Please note, there is very little clearance for turning around.

Hiking Trails: From this point, it's a short 0.2-mile walk down to the viewpoint for Wildhorse Lake. Some hikers—anxious anglers in particular—drop down to the lake via an unmaintained trail.

From the parking area, a 0.5-mile trail climbs to the summit (9,733 feet) where there's a radio repeater station.

Back at the junction, you'll continue around the loop, heading down the mountain from this point on. Rabbitbrush, sagebrush, bitterbrush, and juniper trees grace the slopes and roadway.

1.1 (26.6) **Hiking Trail:** A sign on the left marks the Desert Hiking Trail. An easy hike follows the old jeep road to the south, traveling past a spring, to a rock outcrop at 0.5 mile. From here there's a grand view of Big Indian Gorge, named for the large numbers of Indians that camped in the gorge each summer. According to the late Walt Riddle, who settled on the Little Blitzen River in 1884, the Indians fished, hunted deer and sheep, and gambled, racing their ponies around the bottom of Big Indian.

5.0 (31.6) Rooster Comb area.

4.5 (36.1) **Hiking Trail:** Those choosing to hike into the Little Blitzen Gorge should park somewhere in this area, near the mouth of the Gorge. After wading across the Little Blitzen River, you'll find a trail leading up the Gorge, past the remnants of the old Kuney corral and cabin. Rhubarb still grows by the cabin prompting some hikers to indulge in a little rhubarb jello.

1.5 (37.6) The road improves some as you continue down across a juniper plateau.

2.0 (39.6) Blitzen Crossing.

16.0 (55.6) Reach paved State Highway 205. Turn right and head back to Frenchglen to complete the loop.

10.0 (65.6) Frenchglen.

Malheur National Wildlife Refuge Tour

Although this is a Loop Tour for the most part, you will have to backtrack once you get to the southern end of Malheur National Wildlife Refuge near Frenchglen. No need to worry, however, as there are rooms available at the historic Frenchglen Hotel, camping nearby for both tenters and RVers, and you'll have double the opportunity to see the plentiful wildlife that inhabits the refuge.

The loop begins in Burns, a small town that nearly 3,000 people call home. Located in Harney County, Oregon's largest county with over 10,000 square miles, and one of the largest counties in the U.S., you'll find all amenities with a number of motels and restaurants to choose from.

Burns is a popular place for rockhounds. Area rock dealers estimate that about 20,000 people come to the area annually to collect gemstones. Truly a rockhounder's paradise, Burns is the jumping off point for areas to the south, including the Malheur National Wildlife Refuge, Diamond Craters, and even farther south, Malheur Cave. Before heading out of Burns, there are several places you might want to visit. The Highland Rock Shop is certainly worthy of a stop, as is the Burns Museum where you can learn about the local history.

The Malheur National Wildlife Refuge lies south of town and boasts an enormous population of animal life. Avian species are especially abundant in spring and fall when thousands of birds migrate through the area, following the path of the Pacific Flyway, one of four major North American bird migration routes. Trumpeter swans, the largest of North America's swans, live here year-round, as do those silent creatures of the night, great horned owls.

Some of Harney County's most recent volcanic eruptions can be seen at Diamond Craters, located east of the refuge. Known as one of the finest and most diverse basaltic features in the United States, it lures geologists, scientists, and educators in from around the nation to explore the area.

Geologists estimate that sometime in the last 25,000 years, lava oozed out of the cracked ground to form an enormous pool about six miles in diameter. As the gooey lava hardened, additional molten rock was injected at a shallow depth, lifting up the overlying rock to form the low hills, or domes visible today. More recent volcanic eruptions in the central crater complex are believed to have occurred within the last 1,000 years. Visitors will find a variety of volcanic features including a graben, maars, craters and vents, cinder cones, lava tubes, driblet spires, and spatter cones.

The 17,000-acre geologic wonder is managed by the Bureau of Land Management which is in the process of setting the area up as a natural area. BLM's primary goal is "to help preserve and promote the Diamond Craters as an unusual and unique geologic area." A pamphlet is available for those venturing into the area. Write or call the BLM and ask for your copy of "A self-guided tour of: Diamond Craters—Oregon's Geologic Gem."

This 150-mile tour follows a portion of the Diamond Loop Back Country Byway, a 64-mile loop covering both paved and graveled secondary country roads. An additional 11 miles of dirt road leads to the Kiger Horse Herd Overlook, but it is not officially part of the

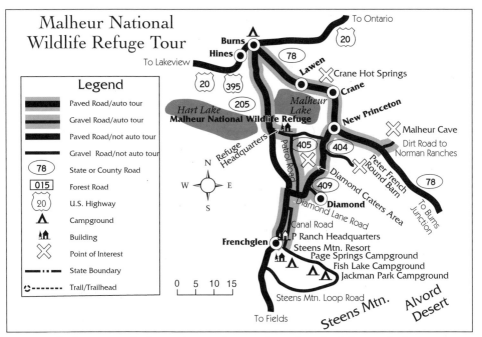

route. High clearance vehicles such as pickup trucks and 4-wheel drive vehicles are necessary for this section of roadway.

For more information contact: Malheur National Wildlife Refuge, Malheur Field Station, Bureau of Land Management (Burns District), or Harney County Visitor Information in Burns, all listed on page 86.

Mileage Log

0.0 (0.0) Junction U.S. 20/U.S. 395/State Highway 78, in downtown Burns. (The Highland Rock Shop is 0.9 mile farther south via U.S. 20/U.S. 395.)

From the junction, go left on paved State Highway 78 (toward Crane).

0.5 (0.5) Junction State Highway 205. This road leads to Frenchglen and Malheur National Wildlife Refuge. If you'd rather do the loop in reverse, hop on Highway 205 at this point.

14.8 (15.3) You'll head through pancake-flat, sagebrush-accented ranch country to the tiny town of Lawen. Lawen consists of a combination post office and store.

8.4 (23.7) Crane Hot Springs, a health resort owned and operated by Jerry Brown who bought the property where the hot springs are located in 1987. Six large tubs—two handicapped accessible—rest in private wooden rooms, fed by well water that registers a toasty 112 degrees. The resort is open year-round, seven days a week, from 8 a.m. until 10 p.m. A pond is available for outside soaking—temperatures range from 95 to 105 degrees.

Four cabins (also handicapped accessible), four electric-only RV sites, and tent sites are also available for those who'd like to stay a while. Future plans for a motel and restaurant are in the works.

3.0 (26.7) Buchanan Junction on the left; keep right toward McDermitt via State Highway 78.

0.4 (27.1) Crane; there's a boarding school and a combination cafe, gas station, and market.

9.0 (36.1) New Princeton; gas station/market. There's a fork just beyond. Those who wish to disregard the trip to Malheur Cave will continue straight (south) on County Road 404 (Lava Beds Road), and skip the following directions.

Side Trip: To reach Malheur Cave, stay left on State Highway 78. You'll pass the Princeton Post Office on the left. Notice the location! Where else but out in the boondocks would you find the post office housed in a tiny shed next to a private mobile home?

After approximately 13.6 miles you'll see a sign for Norman Ranches on the left. Drive through the arch, making a left at the first main fork. The road is good gravel. About 2.9 miles from Highway 78, cross a cattle guard. Make an immediate left, traveling a dusty dirt road that parallels the fence line. Reach the cave in 0.2 mile.

The one-half-mile-long lava tube is owned by Burns Lodge #97 A.F. & A.M. Special permission is needed to enter the cave. Before you go, contact Harney County Visitor Information or Lee Wallace at (541) 573-2677.

2.9 (39.0) Junction County Road 405 (Narrow-Princeton Rd.) which leads to the Malheur National Wildlife Refuge in 9 miles. Keep left.

10.4 (49.4) You'll pass Barton Lake en route to the signed gravel road on the left which leads to the Peter French Round Barn, donated to the Oregon Historical Society by the Jenkins Ranch.

Side Trip: The barn, an architectural marvel and a definite must-see, is a mere 0.9 mile away.

Although the exact date of construction of the barn isn't known, it was in use as early as 1884. Built from native rock and juniper trees, the barn is 100 feet in diameter with a 60-foot circular lava rock corral inside. Twelve enormous juniper trees (no doubt hauled from the bottom of some deep canyon to obtain logs of this size) support the roof with its 50,000 shingles. The center pole is 35 feet high. (With modern equipment, the building of a barn such as this would be a considerable task even by today's standards.)

The barn was built at a time when Peter French, of the famous French-Glenn cattle company, ran several thousand horses. It was used for breaking saddle horses in the winter. In fact, the area between the corral and outer building served as a 20-foot wide paddock for working horses.

4.8 (54.2) Enter the Diamond Craters area. Please note, rock collecting is prohibited in this region.

Side Trip: A self-guiding map is available showing visitors where to drive and describes the unique area accessible via a series of dirt roads.

5.0 (59.2) Reach a T-junction after another 5.0 miles. If you're not interested in the following side trip continue on toward State Highway 205 via Diamond Lane Road.

Side Trip: Go left for 5.5 miles on gravel Diamond Lane Road (County Road 409), also known as Diamond-Grain Camp Road on some maps. The road passes a number of ranches en route to the small town of Diamond. After traveling about halfway to Diamond, you'll pass a turnoff on the right to the McCoy Creek Inn (541-493-2131 or 541-493-2440). Nestled in McCoy Canyon, and home to five generations of the same family, the turn-of-the-century home has been carefully restored. One room is handicapped accessible.

In the town of Diamond, a bustling town of about 50 people when it was a major merchandising outlet for ranchers, sheepsmen, and travelers, you'll find Hotel Diamond (541-493-1898). Newly restored, the hotel was originally built in 1898 by Marion Horton. Used as a private residence after 1940, the restoration process back to a hotel began in 1986.

The bed and breakfast inn offers meals—breakfast and dinner—to hotel guests only. A small deli is open to everyone. A post office and store are located in the same building.

If you'd like to continue on to the Kiger Mustang Viewing Area, continue through Diamond and up the Diamond grade. At the top of the grade, there's a road to the right marked by a sign which indicates the Kiger Mustang Viewing Area. Follow this unmaintained dirt road for approximately 11 miles. A four-wheel drive vehicle is highly recommended.

6.7 (65.9) T-Junction with State Highway 205. Frenchglen is 18 miles south, Burns is 42 miles north.

6.4 (72.3) Make a left on the gravel road which leads to Krumbo Reservoir.

0.2 (72.5) Turn right onto the Canal Road, a dirt road which leads through the refuge.

1.0 (73.5) Benson Pond on the left.

Side Trip: Turn left, following another dirt road 0.3 mile to a welcome stand of cottonwoods, perfect for picnicking. Look for kingfishers, swans, great horned owls, and deer, among other species.

2.1 (75.6) Dredger Pond on the left. Watch for deer, sandhill cranes, and pheasants.

7.0 (82.6) P Ranch Headquarters; facilities include a toilet which you'll see en route to the Long Barn. Look for turkey vultures on the tower.

0.3 (82.9) T-junction: Steens Mountain Road. Frenchglen is 1.5 miles to the right; Page Springs Campground and Steens Mountain Resort are 1.5 miles to the left. (See Steens Mountain Loop Tour for more information.)

To return to Burns, head north, back to the Diamond Lane/State Highway 205 junction (the 65.9-mile mark on this loop). You can reach the junction by returning via the Canal Road or you can head over to Frenchglen and drive north on paved State Highway 205 to the same point.

17.0 (99.9) From the Diamond Lane Road/State Highway 205 junction, turn east (right) onto gravel Diamond Lane.

1.0 (100.9) Turn left onto Patrol Road, a dirt road leading through the refuge.

1.2 (102.1) A dirt road on the left leads to State Highway 205, past the Buena Vista Ponds.

Patrol Road continues past a number of ponds, the Blitzen River, and McLaughlin Slough.

12.3 (114.4) Reach a fork; refuge headquarters is located to the right; the Malheur Field Station is to the left. If you're not interested in the field station, stay right toward headquarters. You'll pass Wright's Pond en route.

3.8 (118.2) Junction. Headquarters is straight ahead 0.4 mile; State Highway 78 is to the right in 16 miles, and State Highway 205 is 6 miles to the left.

From the main gravel road, head west to continue the loop. In about three miles the gravel road turns to paved.

6.0 (124.2) T-Junction: Make a right (go north) on State Highway 205. You'll pass Harney and Malheur Lakes en route to Burns.

23.7 (147.9) T-Junction: Turn left on State Highway 78.

1.7 (149.6) Back to beginning of loop at the main junction (U.S. 20/U.S. 395/State Highway 78) in downtown Burns.

Jordan Valley Area Tour

Spectacular scenes await those who venture off on this excursion through some of Oregon's wildest country. At Three Forks, you can gaze down upon the Owyhee River or you can drive down to the river and soak in a warm springs, hike, or raft the river. Canadian geese make this area their home as well, their gentle honking music for those floating along, camping in, or exploring the steep-walled canyon.

Leslie Gulch. If you like strange and unusual rock formations, then this is the place for you. The gulch was named for Hiram E. Leslie, a pioneer rancher who was struck and killed by lightning there in 1882.

Although you can observe the unique and twisted volcanic tuft formations from the road, why not explore via a series of animal trails which lead throughout several side canyons? Bighorn sheep often graze in the canyon so you'll want to keep an eye out for head-butting rams, delicate ewes, and wide-eyed lambs.

In addition to bighorn sheep, watch for deer, chukar partridge, ravens, western meadowlarks, pigeons, dove, and various raptors including hawks, owls, vultures, eagles, and prairie falcons.

At Succor Creek, explore and/or photograph the massive canyon with its twisted spires and jagged cliffs. Formed 15 million years ago when explosive eruptions deposited the thick volcanic tuff, the area is a virtual potpourri for rockhounds. Interested? If so, you may find calcite crystals, obsidian, petrified wood, and the thunderegg, Oregon's state rock. If you're not into rocks, you can simply relax and enjoy the scene before you, drinking in the symphony of Succor Creek.

Lake Owyhee, a popular spot for anglers, is accessible from Leslie Gulch. You can also reach the lake and points north at Lake Owyhee State Park where fishing (the lake is famous for its bass) and boating are popular.

Snow and mud close portions of the route during the winter months so you'll want to plan your trip accordingly. Spring, summer, and fall are best; mid-April through October is usually the most pleasant although wet, muddy road conditions can occur at any time of the year. Temperatures are moderate in the spring and fall, hot (with highs in the nineties or low 100s), during the summer.

Mileage Log

0.0   (0.0)   From Burns Junction, where U.S. 95 and State Highway 78 merge, go east on paved U.S. 95 North toward Jordan Valley and Boise.

6.1   (6.1)   Bannock War History Marker; water is available. Just ahead you'll cross the Crooked Creek and a variety of cream- and green-colored formations.

6.1   (12.2)   Rome General Store/Cafe/RV Park. There's a telephone across the street.

   Side Trip: Head north via the gravel road which is located across the

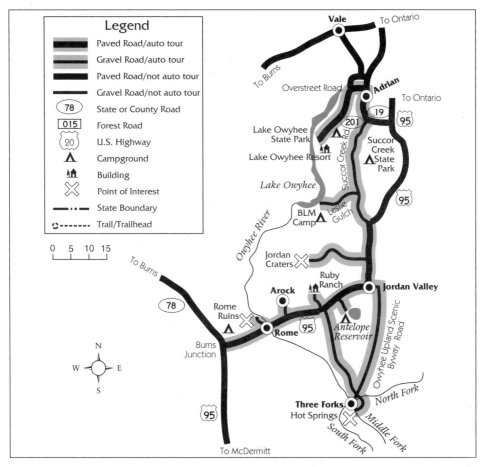

Legend

▬▬▬	Paved Road/auto tour
▬▬▬	Gravel Road/auto tour
▬▬▬	Paved Road/not auto tour
▬▬	Gravel Road/not auto tour
78	State or County Road
015	Forest Road
20	U.S. Highway
▲	Campground
🏠	Building
✕	Point of Interest
—··—	State Boundary
⟲------	Trail/Trailhead

street, near the telephone booth. Drive through a maze of rocks to the 2.1 miles mark. The road curves to the left at this point; drive another 0.9 mile to Rome Coliseum or Rome Ruins as it is also known. The series of gorgeous rock formations resemble ancient Roman architecture, thus the name.

5.4 (17.6) From Rome, continue to this point where there's a signed paved road leading to Arock.

Side Trip: Turn left, traveling through farmland en route to the Arock Post Office and market at 3.3 miles. Continue left on a gravel road to the Fred G. Ranch which is on the right in 1.4 miles. The old pony express station, located on private land, is to the left 0.2 mile. If you'd like to photograph or view the historical site, you can ask for permission at the ranch.

9.5 (27.1) Junction; gravel road heads north (left) toward Danner and Cow Lakes.

Side Trip: From U.S. 95, turnoff onto the gravel road, driving 2.0 miles to a curve in the road. Continue straight another 1.4 miles to an old general store. Danner is 0.2 mile beyond. Ruby Ranch, the oldest building in the county, is to the left. In 1863, a way station began business at the Ruby Ranch. There's a sign and the remains of the Fortified House (Inskip Ranch) nearby. Ahead and to the right is the Charbonne Grave, the burial site of Jean Baptiste Charbonneau, son of renowned Sacajawea.

A stone house in Vale, Oregon, built in 1872.

1.4   28.5)   Turnoff to Three Forks. The gravel road heads southeast for about 33 miles. See "Side Trip To Three Forks" at the end of this mileage log for more information.

1.4   (29.9)   Vale Project Interpretative Site and Taylor Grazing Plaque.

2.2   32.1)   Turnoff to Antelope Reservoir.

           Side Trip: A gravel road leads one mile to the reservoir and a free camping area. There are four picnic tables; toilets and trash bins. Named for the swift and elegant mammals from which the reservoir got its name, pronghorn frequent the area quite regularly.

11.2   (43.3)   Enter Jordan Valley, known for its generations of Basque sheepherders. First settled in 1864 when John Baxter built a hotel and store, the town was once called Baxterville. Today, there are two motels, a market, gas stations, a post office, and an RV Park with a laundromat that is open to the public. Also there are several eating establishments including the Old Basque Inn which serves both Basque and American foods.

           From Jordan Valley, you'll head north on U.S. 95, passing a community park and rodeo arena as you leave town.

8.9   (52.2)   Junction; gravel road leads to Jordan Craters.

           Side Trip: Turn left onto the well-maintained gravel road (which turns to dirt later on) that leads past a series of golden fields to Jordan Craters. After 7.9 miles, there's a creek and a primitive campsite. Continue another

3.2 miles to a fork in the road; make a right. Drive another 6.4 miles to another fork and make a left. You'll reach yet another fork in 5.7 miles; make a left. An extensive lava flow dominates the southern scene as you continue an additional 1.5 miles to an unmarked road which takes off to the left; drive 0.7 mile for a wonderful view of Coffeepot Crater. Continue another 0.6 mile to the crater itself. There's a trail up to the rim for a closer look.

A mere 4,000 years old, Coffeepot Crater was the source of the 20,000-acre lava flow seen today.

10.0 (62.2) Succor Creek parallels the highway at times as you continue up U.S. 95; rolling hills and scattered rock formations add to the scene.

At this point, turn left on Succor Creek Road, pioneer stage road of old, and a Back Country Byway at present. The road is signed for Succor Creek State Park, but also leads to Leslie Gulch. The well-maintained gravel road deteriorates as you near Succor Creek.

8.1 (70.3) Road curves to the left.

1.8 (72.1) Junction: Make a left to go to Leslie Gulch. If you'd rather skip driving the 14.1 miles to Lake Owyhee via Leslie Gulch (I wouldn't recommend it), jump to the 100.3-mile mark. The drive from here leads one through a series of rolling hills that become more rugged and interesting as you head west.

6.9 79.0) The scene only becomes more impressive (if possible) as you begin your descent into Leslie Gulch. Grades can be 11% at times so large motorhomes and trailers are not recommended. Please note: Flash floods can be a problem at times. Use caution. Remember, this is the only road in or out of the area.

2.6 (81.6) There are toilets and an interpretative sign about the bighorn sheep that frequent the area. Also there's a picnic area and road leading to Dago Canyon on the left just prior to this point.

4.1 (85.7) No fee campground on the left; there are toilets and picnic tables. Also a waste water disposal.

0.5 (86.2) Lake Owyhee. There's a boat ramp and toilets.

To continue the loop, drive back to the junction at the 72.1-miles mark.

14.1 (100.3) Junction: Continue north from this point to Succor Creek. Although the dirt road is usually in fine shape, it is rutted in sections so please use care when driving it. You'll pass a couple of side roads as you travel; remember to keep to the right and you shouldn't lose your way. The road eventually descends to the Succor Creek drainage with its massive pinnacles and rock outcroppings.

9.8 (110.1) Succor Creek State Park; toilets, water, picnic tables. This is a self-service fee area with 19 primitive sites.

Continue north through a maze of rugged cliffs which give way to gentle hills as you descend. The road is good and only improves as you head north.

15.4 (125.5) Succor Creek Road merges onto paved State Highway 201/State Highway 19. The road continues in a northern direction with signs pointing the way to Adrian. A patchwork of crops—turnips, sugar beets, corn, potatoes, onions, and mustard seed—decorate the land as you continue north.

7.9 (133.4) Reach the small town of Adrian, population 150. Located along the Snake River, there's a cafe, a post office, and the C & J Market which boasts of a

Hiker and Samoyed near Hot Springs along Owyhee River near Three Forks.

grill in addition to groceries.

2.0 (135.4)   Junction Overstreet Road. Make a left on this paved road which leads to Lake Owyhee State Park.

5.2 (140.6)   Make a left onto the unsigned paved road (although a road name is missing, there is a sign for Lake Owyhee State Park).

3.3 (143.9)   Snively's Hot Springs is just off the road on the left. It's a beautiful drive along the Owyhee River as you continue, a place where towering rock formations add personality to the scene. Primitive camp sites are available throughout the area.

12.2 (156.1)   Reach the dam/spillway at this point.

2.4 (158.5)   Gordon Gulch Picnic area. This shaded site provides picnic tables, grills, toilets, water, and a boat ramp. Best of all, there's a fabulous view of the lake.

1.2 (159.7)   Owhyee State Park Campground—V.W. McCormack Area. This lovely shaded camp (with some open sites) offers three hot water showers, toilets, picnic tables, grills, a fish cleaning area, a boat ramp, and electric hookups. Anglers try for copious amounts of trout, catfish, bass, and crappie.

1.1 (160.8)   Lake Owyhee Resort; a private RV park offering sites with water and electricity. Also, there's a motel, cabins, a tackle shop, a restaurant, a bar, and a store. Boat rentals are available as well.

Side Trip To Three Forks

Three Forks can be a busy place in the spring and fall. During the spring, it is a primary take-out and put-in site for floatboat trips along the upper and middle sections of the Owyhee River. In the fall, hunters use Three Forks as a base camp.

Although Three Forks is a definite must-see in my book, a place where fish leap, and Canada geese, yellow-headed blackbirds, ravens, doves, and golden eagles wing their way through the canyon, there are those who will choose to forego the side trip, opting instead to remain on U.S. 95 to Jordan Valley. Actually, both drives are nice. If you stay on U.S. 95, you'll have the chance to visit Antelope Reservoir. If you head south to Three Forks, however, you'll merge back onto the main route at Jordan Valley. If you don't want to miss a thing, you can retrace your tracks and head back to the starting point for the side trip.

From the 28.5-mile mark on the main route (which is listed as mile 0.0 below), turn right onto the dirt road leading the way to Three Forks. Although the road is dirt, it is passable in all types of vehicles as long as the weather is good.

0.0   (0.0)   Junction U.S. 95 and the dirt road leading to Three Forks.

16.5   (16.5)   Owyhee Canyon Overlook turnoff on the right.

     Side Trip: A great view of the canyon is only 0.2 mile away.

11.8   (28.3)   Fork; Jordan Valley is 33 miles to the left; Three Forks is 6 miles to the right; keep right to Three Forks, descending to the bottom of the canyon.

4.2   (32.5)   Reach the bottom of the canyon at Three Forks, named for the South, Middle, and North Owyhee Rivers which converge here. The South and Middle fork meet here; the North Fork greets the Middle Fork about 0.5 mile upstream.

     There's a toilet and plenty of room for tent camping. A barn with hay, a cabin with cots, and a wood stove for cooking and heat, is also located at the base of the canyon, but it is not available for public use.

     According to Jerry Taylor, Jordan Resource Area Manager, the cabin and corral were constructed by a local rancher many years ago to "facilitate trailing livestock through the area." Because the facilities were never properly authorized, there are existing legal and liability questions surrounding the complex thus BLM cannot offer them for public use. Plans are currently in effect to resolve this situation.

     Side Trip: There's a 2.6-mile side trip to a couple of warm springs located along the Middle Fork of the Owyhee River. From the junction near the barn and road at Three Forks, drive east past the barn. Cross a bridge over the North Fork Owyhee River in 0.5 mile and continue to the right. Drive another two miles or so to the top of a hill then descend to two warm springs. This is a good place to park if you have two-wheel drive as a four-wheel drive is probably necessary to descend the road from this point.

     The warm springs are 200 yards or less from the top of the hill. They are privately owned; BLM suggests visitors get the owner's permission before using them.

4.2   (36.7)   From the junction at Three Forks, head back up the canyon to the junction you passed previously, the one at the 28.3-miles mark. Keep to the right unless you want to head back to the same point where you turned off of U.S. 95 (the 28.5-mile mark). Both roads are gravel.

9.5   (46.2)   Fork; keep left, now traveling the Owyhee Uplands Scenic Byway Road. Pass several ranches en route, entering Idaho some place along the way.

14.4   (60.6)   Road turns to pavement.

7.6   (68.2)   Junction U.S. 95 in Jordan Valley. This point is near the 43.5-mile mark on the primary mileage log.

Alvord Desert Loop Tour

From the tiny hamlet of Fields, to the vast Alvord Basin with its magnificent views of the abrupt eastern side of Steens Mountain, this loop provides something for everyone. Those who enjoy viewing the scenery from their vehicle, will have plenty to see without getting out of the car. But those who enjoy getting out and about may want to spend days or even weeks visiting the Trout Creek Mountains, the Pueblo Mountains, the Sheepshead Mountains, and there are numerous side canyons dissecting the Steens to explore as well. In addition, there's always the Alvord Valley and its hot springs and lakes. Known as the "truest desert area within Oregon," the Alvord Basin as it is also known, was once the site of a vast prehistoric lake. Modern travelers can still view a series of small, relic lakes, fish a number of streams, and enjoy the warmth of a number of hot springs.

Fed by hot springs rich in sodium borate, Borax Lake was the source of a borax industry around 1900. Used in cleaning agents, Chinese laborers collected, processed, bagged, and shipped the crystals by 16-mule-team wagon to Winnemucca, Nevada, about 130 miles south.

Animal life in the desert may seem bleak and nearly nonexistent, but it is there if you only spend the time to find it. Drive along deserted roads in the late evening and early morning hours, and you might see coyotes or jackrabbits. Scope the cliffs of surrounding mountains and you might spot a bighorn sheep or two. Walk across the desert and horned lizards, better known as "horny toads" may be your companions. There are two species native to Oregon, the short-horned lizard which is a protected species in Oregon, and the desert horned lizard. Like all horned lizards, they have short tails, and wide, flat bodies. Ants are their favorite food, although they will feed on spiders and other insects.

Provisions are rare along this loop with Fields and Burns Junction the only places offering gas, food, and lodging. Fields is a ranching community, some of these ranches of which have been owned and operated by the same family for generations. Established in 1881 by Charles Fields, the town consists of a few homes and a two-room school, as well as a combination store, cafe, gas station, campground, hotel, and post office. Burns Junction has similar amenities.

Mileage Log

0.0 (0.0) Fields-Denio Road (County Road 201) is a paved road in Fields, but just north of town it branches off onto a well-maintained gravel road. The road skirts past sagebrush and numerous jackrabbits (usually seen early and late in the day and night). The road name is unsigned when heading north, but there is a sign pointing the way to Andrews.

12.7 (12.7) Town of Andrews. Founded in 1890 when a post office was established, the once bustling community now consists of a one-room schoolhouse and several homes. Pass Wildhorse Lake Ranch and Mann Lake Ranch along the way.

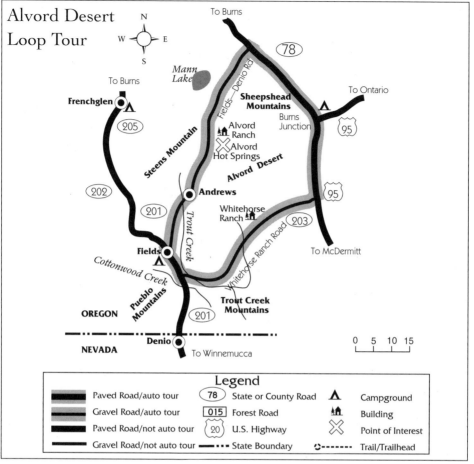

Alvord Desert Loop Tour

Legend

Paved Road/auto tour	(78) State or County Road	▲ Campground
Gravel Road/auto tour	[015] Forest Road	🏠 Building
Paved Road/not auto tour	(20) U.S. Highway	✕ Point of Interest
Gravel Road/not auto tour	━ ━ ·· State Boundary	⚲------- Trail/Trailhead

6.1 (18.8) A spur road on the right leads to a fine place for camping near the desert floor. Also, there's a warm spring near here, but it's closer to the road than the desert.

      For an unique experience, walk out onto the desert floor at night (full moon nights are best), and feel the overwhelming sense of solitude, the vastness of the desert.

2.4 (21.2) Alvord Desert Hot Springs. There's an outdoor pool and an enclosed one for private bathing. No soap please.

5.6 (26.8) Alvord Ranch.

5.6 (32.4) A dirt road on the left leads to Mann Lake; there's another access road in 0.7 mile. There are pit toilets at this scenic spot, named for an early rancher. It is a favorite fishing spot where anglers vie for rainbow and cutthroat trout.

      You'll see the highest point of the Steens from this point; the Sheepshead Mountains are to the east.

8.1 (40.5) There's a dry lake and remnants of an old building on the right.

2.1 (42.6) Dry lake.

1.7 (44.3) Juniper Ranch.

3.9 (48.2) Dry lake.

Hiker at sunrise, looking west from a butte
into Cottonwood Creek drainage between Fields and Denio.

Alvord Desert Hot Springs before 1992 refurbishing.

6.9 (55.1) Junction paved State Highway 78; make a right. As you continue, lumpy lava formations dot the landscape and range cattle may share the road.

18.7 (73.8) Entering Mountain Time.

7.1 (80.9) Junction US 95. Burns Junction has a combination RV Park, motel, tire service, cafe, and gas station.

12.2 (93.1) Back to Pacific Standard Time.

8.6 (101.7) Turn right on Harney County Road 203 (Whitehorse Ranch Road), a maintained gravel road. If you were to continue south on U.S. 95 instead of turning, you'd end up in McDermitt, 34 miles south. McDermitt is a small gambling town with a couple of motels, gas stations, cafe, fast food establishment, library, post office, and gambling machines. The Santa Rosa Mountains provide a magnificent backdrop.

7.8 (109.5) Coyote Lake is visible from the top of the rise.

13.4 (122.9) Whitehorse Ranch. The oldest ranch in the area, Whitehorse Ranch is nestled in view of Steens Mountain. Much has been written about the ranch located on Whitehorse Creek. It is believed the ranch was named "for a beautiful white horse ridden by an Indian chief who frequented that section in the early days."

According to a Malheur County Historical Society sign at the ranch, the site was once the location of Camp C.F. Smith. The camp was established May 1866 to protect Oregon Central Military Road. It was abandoned in November, 1869, and subsequently ranched by John S. Devine.

18.8 (141.7) Trout Creek flows through the narrow canyon amid rock outcrops. Watch for coyotes, western meadowlarks, quail, ravens, turkey vultures, and more as you move dream-like through the picture-perfect scene.

7.7 (149.4) Junction with the Fields-Denio Road (County Road 201), a paved road. Make a right and head north to Fields, thereby completing the loop.

0.3 (149.7) Cottonwood Creek.

Side Trip: A dirt road leads 0.3 mile to the left to a good spot for camping or hiking.

4.9 (154.6) This is the approximate mileage from the junction to Fields.

Sheldon National Wildlife Refuge Tour

Although this trip begins in the small town of Plush, you can actually start out in Lakeview, about 31 miles west of Adel. Adel is located about 18 miles south of Plush. En route, you'll dip down into Nevada, skirting the northern edge of Sheldon National Wildlife Refuge along the way. You'll want to find the time to stop here before venturing on to Fields. (See chapter on the Sheldon National Wildlife Refuge for more information.)

Mileage Log

0.0 (0.0) Downtown Plush. (For more information on Plush, see the Hart Mountain Tour.)

0.4 (0.4) Junction CR 3-10 and CR 3-13. Head south on CR 3-10 to Adel. As you depart from Plush, you'll see Hart Lake off to the left. It's a beautiful drive as you continue south with ranchland and marshland to the east, sagebrush, rocks, and rugged cliffs to the west. Juniper trees dot the land. Farther south, look for Crump Lake to the east.

14.9 (15.3) Pelican Lake. The privately owned lake offers refuge to 125 pairs of nesting American white pelicans. It is also home for numerous gulls, great blue herons, egrets, killdeer, and curlews.

2.6 (17.9) Junction Highway 140 at Adel. There's a grill, groceries, gasoline, and other miscellaneous items for sale. There's also an RV park and post office. The combination store/station was constructed in 1897 by A.J. Monroe. It originally served as a general store; later is was used as a post office and saddlery.

As you exit Adel, head east across Greaser Flat.

5.1 (23.0) Junction BLM 6132, a dusty, dirt road on the left.

Side Trip: Follow BLM 6132 to Greaser Petroglyph which is on the right in 0.7 mile.

Although their meaning and/or function have yet to be determined, we do know that petroglyphs are actual rock drawings that were carved or pecked into the surface. Pictographs, on the other hand, are drawings painted on rocks.

10.4 (33.4) Cross Blizzard Gap at an elevation of 6,122 feet.

6.1 (39.5) Dirt road on the left leads to Guano Lake.

6.5 (46.0) Long 8% grade leads to the 6,240-foot level at Doherty Rim Summit. There's a flat area for enjoying the view.

6.4 (52.4) Harney County line.

2.6 (55.0) Enter Nevada, the Silver State, and the Sheldon National Wildlife Refuge. Dust devils, an occasional ranch house, sagebrush, and other plant species are friends as you travel along.

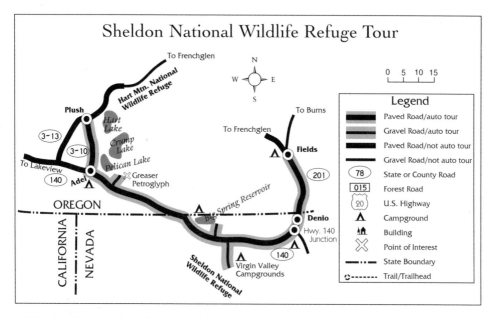

Sheldon National Wildlife Refuge Tour

10.9 (65.9) Gravel road on the left leads to Big Spring Reservoir Campground.

Side Trip: You'll travel 2.5 miles to the camp area where there are toilets. Numerous species of birds live at the lake.

8.2 (74.1) Turnoff (to the south) on gravel road leads to signed Royal Peacock Mines and Sheldon National Wildlife Refuge sub-headquarters.

Side Trip: Travel past sub-headquarters which is known as the Dufurrena field station, and notice the buildings (built in the early 1900s) which are made of sandstone blocks. Hugh Null, refuge manager, says many of the buildings on the refuge were made using sandstone. Although it shut down in 1965, at one time there was a sandstone quarry located near the field station. Of equal interest is the barn with its willow corrals, built around 1900.

Look for Thousand Creek Gorge on the left as you travel toward Virgin Valley Campground, 2.4 miles from State Highway 140. There's a bathhouse and outdoor swimming pool, but no nude swimming is allowed. There is, however, a bathhouse for private baths. Picnic tables and toilets are provided at no charge.

24.9 (99.0) Highway 140 Junction; truck stop with a cafe, motel, RV Park, gasoline, propane, groceries, and gambling machines/slot machines.

2.4 (101.4) Head north to Denio, Nevada, via paved Fields-Denio Road, Harney County 201. Post office, Bar/Inn, school.

13.2 (114.6) Gravel road on the right leads to McDermitt and Trout Creek. This junction is just past Tum Tum Lake.

0.3 (114.9) Cottonwood Creek.

Side Trip: Cross the creek via a dirt road, continuing up the creek for about 0.3 mile. At this point the road narrows to a jeep road. There's a nice area for camping.

4.9 (119.8) Fields; combination store, cafe, gas station, campground, hotel, and post office.

Tour Connectors

T he following tour connectors are meant for exactly what you might think—they connect one tour with another. For instance, those traveling the Hart Mountain Tour might use the first connector, Frenchglen to Fields, thereby connecting with the Alvord Desert Loop Tour. Or, maybe you'd rather use the connector to get to Fields to do the Plush to Fields Tour in reverse. Mix and match, use the tour connectors any way you choose.

Frenchglen To Fields

0.0   (0.0)   Frenchglen. Head south on paved State Highway 205.

10.0   (10.0)   Junction Steens Mountain Loop Road and State Highway 205.

4.9   (14.9)   Pass the Roaring Springs Ranch. At this point the road is now called State Highway 202. As you continue along, the scene is painted with rugged Catlow Rim to the east and a series of endless fields to the west.

22.5   (37.4)   State Highway 202 climbs then descends, carving a pass where Catlow Rim meets the Pueblo Mountains. Notice Steens Mountain as you continue.

12.0   (49.4)   Junction; this route (which leads to State Highway 78) takes off to the left through the Alvord Desert. See the Fields/Alvord Desert/Burns Junction Loop for more information.

         If you keep to the right, you'll reach the tiny town of Fields, established in 1881, in a short distance.

View to the south from butte near Cottonwood Creek.

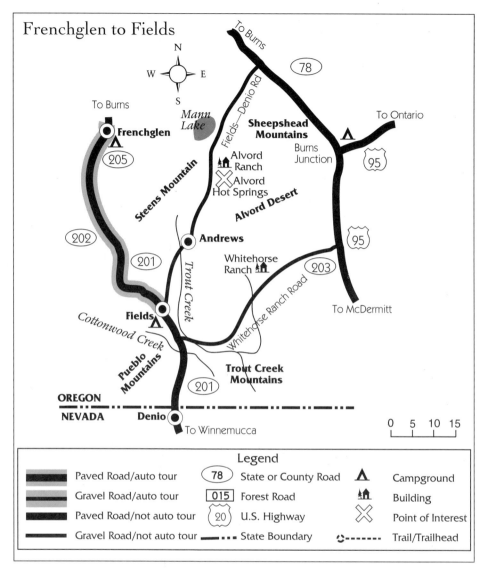

Frenchglen to Fields

To Burns

78

To Ontario

To Burns

Mann Lake

Sheepshead Mountains

Burns Junction

95

Frenchglen

205

Alvord Ranch

Alvord Hot Springs

Steens Mountain

Alvord Desert

202

Andrews

95

201

Whitehorse Ranch

203

Trout Creek

Whitehorse Ranch Road

To McDermitt

Fields

Cottonwood Creek

Pueblo Mountains

Trout Creek Mountains

201

OREGON

NEVADA Denio

To Winnemucca

0 5 10 15

Legend

▬▬	Paved Road/auto tour	78	State or County Road	▲	Campground
▬▬	Gravel Road/auto tour	015	Forest Road	🏠	Building
▬▬	Paved Road/not auto tour	20	U.S. Highway	✕	Point of Interest
—	Gravel Road/not auto tour	—▪▪▪	State Boundary	⟲------	Trail/Trailhead

Lake Owhyee State Park To Burns (via Vale)

From Lake Owyhee State Park, you'll venture north through the Snake River Valley. An agricultural hub, the communities of Vale, Nyssa, and Ontario, produce crops of mint, corn, sugar beets, wheat, alfalfa, onions, fruits, potatoes, and much more.

As you near Vale, you'll enter into the world of the Old Oregon Trail. In 1841 hardy emigrants began the arduous journey west, traveling from Independence, Missouri, to Oregon City, Oregon, following the first overland trail. For more than 20 years, thousands of determined pioneers made the journey, all of whom dreamed of settling in the West. Many died along the way, though, so many in fact that the trail was often called the "longest graveyard."

Lake Owyhee State Park to Burns

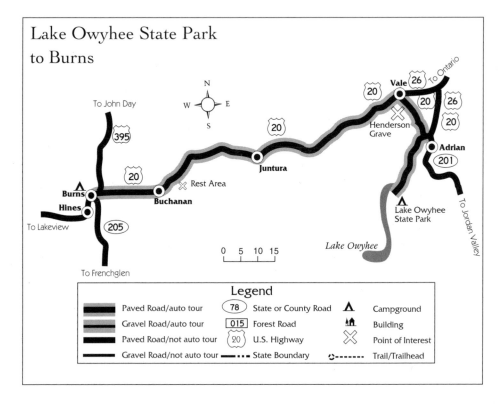

0.0   (0.0)   Lake Owyhee State Park. (It's Mountain Time in this area.)

19.1 (19.1) Junction with Overstreet Road which leads east to Adrian. Stay straight (north).

3.1   (22.2) Go right on Owyhee Ave. then make an immediate left (in 100 yards or so) on Norwood Drive.

1.0   (23.2) Junction Klamath Ave.; make a right.

1.0   (24.2) Junction Lytle Ave.; turn left towards Vale.

0.5   (24.7) Make a right on Janeta Ave. (If you're interested in a place to camp, make a left and follow the signs to Cow Hollow Park, about 0.2 mile away.

0.2   (24.9) Make a left on Lytle Blvd. Sunset Market is on the corner. They boast of a grill, gas, and groceries.

2.6   (27.5) Junction Enterprise Ave. As you continue from here to Vale, you are actually traveling on the old Oregon Trail. Because you are traveling on BLM (public) land, feel free to walk the trail. It's 12 miles to Vale.

5.0   (32.5) Keeney Historic Site. You'll learn about the Trail and its hardships from this interpretive site where wagon ruts are still visible.

5.7   (38.2) Junction Sand Hollow Rd.

              Side Trip: Go left then right at the first fork. Henderson Grave (it is marked) is 0.2 mile away and easy to find. The grave represents one of thousands who died on the trail.

0.8   (39.0) Cross the Malheur River just before reaching the U.S. Highway 20 junction in downtown Vale. On a cool day you might see steam billowing off of the river as hot water breaks into the river at this point. Be sure to test the

Owyhee Lake at sunset, Owyhee State Park.

Burns to Lakeview

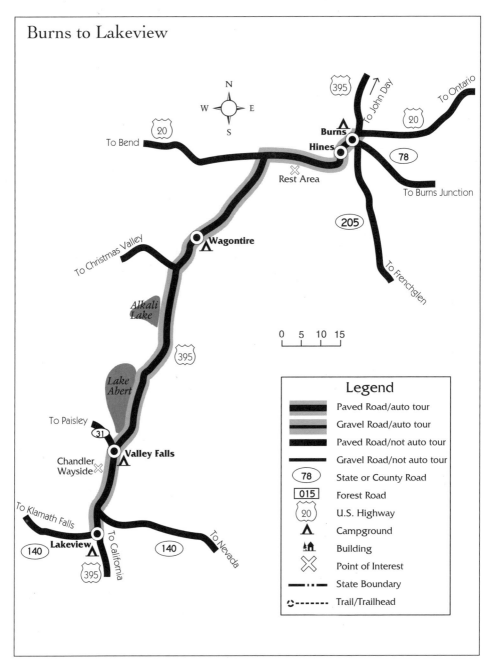

water temperature before entering. In some places the water can burn.

Side Trip: Look for the Stone House at the corner of Main St. and C St. The unique house, listed on the National Register of Historic Places, was built in 1872 by Louis B. Rinehart. At one time the agricultural community was called Stone House, but the name was changed to Vale (meaning "valley") when the post office was established.

Make a left on U.S. Highways 20 and 26. You'll find all amenities in town.

Side Trip: If you drive to the right a short ways you'll see East Entrance Park at the Stephen Meeks Cutoff. Here you'll find water, toilets, and picnic tables. A commemorative plaque states, "In 1845 Meek led 200 families away from the Oregon Trail seeking a shorter route west. Gold found en route began the Blue Bucket Legend. Hardship drove the train back to the Oregon Trail at The Dalles."

Obviously, Vale was a popular resting place for weary travelers of the Oregon Trail. Today, quilted fields of potatoes, onions, sugar beets, and other crops delight those who enjoy traveling through farmland.

0.6	(39.6)	West Entrance Park.
55.2	(94.8)	Juntura; a small oasis with a cafe, store, motels, gas, and a restaurant.
9.5	(104.3)	Enter Pacific Standard Time.
23.9	(128.2)	Rest area; open November 1 through April 1; there's shade, toilets, picnic tables.
1.0	(129.2)	Buchanan: There's a free museum with many items from the local area. Also there's a gift shop with snacks and other items for sale, including a fine array of gemstone jewelry and a wide assortment of superbly crafted Indian jewelry and crafts.
21.5	(150.7)	Enter the outskirts of Burns, home to a large wood products company (stocked by the Blue Mountains to the north), and the nucleus of the area's cattle industry. All services are available as you continue.
0.4	(151.1)	Burns Chamber of Commerce and Harney County Historical Museum on the right. Located on West D Street, the chamber is open Monday through Friday, from 9 a.m. to 5 p.m. The museum is open June through September; hours are Tuesday through Fridays 9 a.m. to 5 p.m., Saturdays 9 a.m. to noon. Relics include artifacts from local pioneer families and an extensive photo collection of early Burns and surrounding areas.
1.4	(152.5)	Junction U.S. 20/U.S. 395/State Highway 78 in downtown Burns.

Burns To Lakeview

0.0	(0.0)	Junction U.S. 20/U.S. 395/State Highway 78 in downtown Burns. Go straight on U.S. 20/U.S. 395, passing the Highland Rock Shop along the way. Inside, you'll see a rock fire place which took eight years to complete. Faced with 80% Oregon rock, most of the rocks are machine polished. The shop is also a showcase for the many types of rocks—Burns obsidian, agate, Buchanan thundereggs, for example—found in the Burns area.
1.4	(1.4)	Enter Hines, founded in 1929, when construction of the Edward Hines Lumber Company mill began. As you pass through the all-service town, you'll see the Valley Golf Club on the left. As you exit town, there are RV spaces in a mobile home park on the left.
4.1	(5.5)	Bureau of Land Management office.
11.7	(17.2)	Rest area on the left; there's a nature trail here.
9.2	(26.4)	Riley; post office. Just beyond, U.S. 395 branches off toward Lakeview. Make a left.
28.2	(54.6)	Wagontire. This tiny town of two offers a motel, gas pumps, cafe, and RV park with full hookups.
18.5	(73.1)	Sand dunes on the right.

Sign greeting visitors from both ends of Lakeview.

Geese at Perpetual Geyser in Lakeview, Oregon.

2.9 (76.0) Alkali Lake; you'll find a cafe and gas at this tiny establishment.

22.5 (98.5) There are fine views of Lake Abert as you travel the east side of Lake County's largest body of water. Although the lake has no known fish population, it attracts thousands of migratory birds each year, and supports a brine shrimp population, some of which is harvested each year for fish food. It also provides nesting habitat for the snowy plover, a sensitive bird species.

Paralleling the lake is Abert Rim, home to a herd of about 100 bighorn sheep. According to geologists, the 30-mile long fault scarp which towers more than 2,000 feet above the lake, is the largest exposed fault in North America.

17.5 (116.0) Reach the junction of State Highway 31 at Valley Falls. There are groceries, gas, an RV Park, and cabins.

5.0 (121.0) Chandler State Park on the right. Located along Crooked Creek, this picnic area has water and restrooms. The road leading through the park merges back onto U.S. 395.

12.8 (133.8) Junction State Highway 140. Westbound State Highway 140 merges onto U.S. 395 at this point. Continue south on U.S. 395/State Highway 140.

4.7 (138.5) Downtown Lakeview.

Resources

Bureau of Land Management
Burns District Office
HC-74 12533 Hwy. 20 West
Hines, OR 97738
(541) 573-4400

Bureau of Land Management
Vale District
100 Oregon Street
Vale, OR 97918
(541) 473-3144

Desert Trail Association
P.O. Box 537
Burns, OR 97720

**Frenchglen Hotel/State
Historical Wayside**
Frenchglen Hotel
Frenchglen, OR 97736
(541) 493-2825

Harney County Visitor Information
18 W. "D" St.
Burns, OR 97720
(541) 573-2636

**Hart Mountain
National Antelope Refuge**
Refuge Manager
P.O. Box 111
Lakeview, OR 97630
(541) 947-3315

Idaho Outfitters Guide Association
P.O. Box 95
Boise, ID 83701
(208) 342-1919

Lake County Chamber of Commerce
513 Center Street - Courthouse
Lakeview, OR 97630
(541) 947-6040

Lakeview Ranger District
524 North G Street
Lakeview, OR 97630
(541) 947-2151

Malheur County Chamber of Commerce
173 S.W. First St.
Ontario, OR 97914
(541) 889-8012

Malheur Field Station
HCR 72, Box 260
Princeton, OR 97721
(541) 493-2629

Malheur National Wildlife Refuge
HC-72, P.O. Box 245
Princeton, OR 97721
(541) 493-2323

Oregon Guides and Packers Association
P.O. Box 10841
Eugene, OR 97440
(541) 683-9552

Plush "Diamond" Works
P.O. Box 50
Plush, OR 97637
(541) 947-3194

Sheldon National Wildlife Refuge
Refuge Manager
P.O. Box 111
Lakeview, OR 97630
(541) 947-3315

Steens Mountain Camper Corral
Frenchglen, OR 97736
(541) 493-2415

Vale Chamber of Commerce
Box 660
Vale, OR 97918
(541) 473-3800

Acknowledgments

Donna Ikenberry. Stephanie Hakanson photo.

As a single woman I'm often asked how I like traveling alone. I guess I don't think too much about being alone because I know God is by my side, carrying me through the tough spots, giving me comfort and support on a day-to-day basis. ·

It's also difficult to feel lonely when you have a family such as mine. I am extremely proud of my parents, Donald and Beverly Ikenberry, and my brothers, Don and David Ikenberry. Although miles often separate us, they are in my heart always. Some people ask what my family thought when I sold my home and almost all of my belongings to go on the road full-time. I'm honored to say they stuck by me— believing in me when I only sold two photographs and made $70 that first year—showering me with their endless love and support. God knows I couldn't love them more.

My Samoyed Sam accompanied me on most of my journeys to southeast Oregon, flashing me a handsome "smile" at every opportunity. Although Sam died in 1993, he continues to travel with me in spirit.

I have many friends to thank for making my travels special. It seems as though new friends pop up wherever I go, friends that urge me to come back to their area, friends that stay in touch even when I'm far away. A special thanks goes to both my old friends and my new ones—I'm grateful for your warmth, your smiles, your love.

Numerous government agencies gladly answered all of my questions and provided me with a big sack of research material. To all of you, I give my sincere thanks.

I've dedicated *Oregon's Outback* to Oral Bullard. Oral will always have a special place in my heart for he was my first book publisher and the genius behind this book idea.

When I started traveling full-time in 1983, I had but one dream—to sell my photographs, images if you will, to magazine, book, and calendar companies. The following year I read that if a person can write as well as photograph they have a better chance of selling their work. Thus, I started my writing career.

I'd only written and sold a couple of pieces when I bought my first backpacking equipment in 1985. A few months later I thought it might be fun to write a book about Oregon's wilderness areas. I imagined hiking the trails in all 36 preserves and writing a guidebook for others to do the same. One day I mailed off a query to Oral at The Touchstone Press. Within a couple of months we had discussed the idea and I was signing my first book contract.

Oral never bothered to ask what kind of experience I had: He didn't know I had but three days of backpacking experience. He didn't ask how many articles I'd sold: At the time, I would have said three. To his credit, Oral took a chance and I ended up writing a series of four guidebooks on Oregon's wilderness areas. (These books are now available from Frank Amato Publications.)

I will always be grateful to Oral for giving me a chance based on what I was willing to do, not what I had done. When he asked me to write this book on southeast Oregon, I jumped at the chance. When he died of cancer this book was still in the planning stages, and I immediately knew that I would dedicate it to him for he loved Oregon's high desert. Thanks, Oral.

Before closing I must give an additional thanks to Kathy Johnson and the others at Frank Amato Publications. Working with them has been a delight.

Other Oregon Wilderness Books by Donna Ikenberry

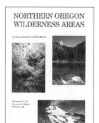

Northern Oregon Wilderness Areas

Donna Ikenberry Aitkenhead

37 beautiful short to long hikes in these Wilderness areas: Badger Creek, Bull of the Woods, Columbia, Middle Santiam, Mt. Hood, Mt. Jefferson, Salmon/ Huckleberry, Table Rock. 6 x 9 inches, 112 pages.
SB: $12.95   ISBN: 0-911518-87-8

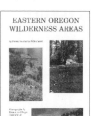

Eastern Oregon Wilderness Areas

Donna Ikenberry Aitkenhead

39 beautiful short to long hikes in these Wilderness areas: Black Canyon, Bridge Creek, Eagle Cap, Hells Canyon, Mill Creek, Monument Rock, North Fork John Day, North Fork Umatilla, Strawberry Mountain, Wenaha-Tucannon. 6 x 9 inches, 112 pages.
SB: $12.95   ISBN: 0-911518-81-9

Central Oregon Wilderness Areas

Donna Ikenberry Aitkenhead

41 beautiful short to long hikes in these Wilderness areas: Cummins Creek, Diamond Peak, Drift Creek, Menagerie, Mt. Washington, Rock Creek, Three Sisters, Waldo Lake. 6 x 9 inches, 112 pages.
SB: $12.95   ISBN: 0-911518-83-5

Southern Oregon Wilderness Areas

Donna Aitkenhead

35 beautiful short to long hikes in these Wilderness areas: Boulder Creek, Gearhart Mountain, Grassy Knob, Kalmiopsis, Mountain Lakes, Mount Thielsen, Red Buttes, Rogue-Umpqua Divide, Sky Lakes, Wild Rogue. 6 x 9 inches, 112 pages.
SB: $12.95   ISBN: 0-911518-78-9

To Order: Inquire at your local book store
or contact Frank Amato Publications, Inc. — 503•653•8108
P.O. Box 82112, Portland, Oregon 97282